For the Lord thy God bringeth thee

into a good land,

a land of brooks of water,

of fountains and depths that spring

out of valleys and hills:

(Deut. 8-7-8)

THIS IS ISRAEL

Pictorial Guide & Souvenir

by Sylvia Mann

Produced by Palphot Ltd.

ACKNOWLEDGEMENTS:

We are grateful to all those who assisted in the publication of this up-to-date Guide, photographers, publishers, The Israel Museum, Jerusalem, the Holyland Corporation, Jerusalem, and other Museums and Institutions.

Maps:

Copyright by Carta, Jerusalem — pp. 3, 7, 8, 16, 24, 39, 65, 84, 89 122, 138, 150.

Copyright by Amir Publishers — pp. 18, 110.

Other Pictorial Guides published by Palphot Ltd.
Available in most European languages

The Holy Land
The Holy Land I Love by David Roberts
Our Visit to Jerusalem
The Bedouins
Bethlehem
Caesarea
The Dome of the Rock, Jerusalem
Eilat and Sinai
The Garden Tomb, Jerusalem
Hai Bar, Eilat
Our Visit to a Kibbutz
Masada
Megiddo
Nazareth, The Church of the Annunciation
The Sea of Galilee
The Model of Ancient Jerusalem
Flowers of the Holy Land
Akko, St. Jean d'Acre
Yad Vashem
Egypt by David Roberts

ISBN 965-280-000-7

ISRAEL

Mediterranean Sea

SYRIA

Golan

Galilee

Haifa

Samaria

Tel Aviv-Yafo

JERUSALEM

AMMAN

J O R D A N

Negev

Sinai

Suez

Gulf of Suez

E G Y P T

Gulf of Eilat

Eilat • **Aqaba**

S A U D I
A R A B I A

Red Sea

LEGEND
Boundary	
Town	
Village	
Historical Site	
Road	
Railway	
Harbour	
Airfield	

All heights are in meters

0   20   40   60 km

Carta, Jerusalem

CONTENTS :

Introduction: History, Geography and General Information   5-14

I **Jerusalem** ....
   Historical background   16-18
   The Old City — the Gates and Walls; the Temple Mount; the Western Wall; Via Dolorosa; Mount Zion; Mount Scopus and the Mount of Olives   19-48
   New Jerusalem — Mishkenot Sha'ananim; Mea · Shearim and other quarters; shopping in town; the President's Residence; the Cultural Centre; Mount Herzl and Yad ve'Shem; the Hebrew University; Hadassah Medical Centre and the model of Second Temple Jerusalem   49-64

II **Southward from Jerusalem** — to Bethlehem; Solomon's Pools; Kfar Etzion; Hebron and Beersheba   66-76

III **Eastward from Jerusalem** — to the Judean Desert; Jericho; Qumran; Ein Gedi; Masada; Ein Bokek and Sdom   77-88

IV **The Jordan Valley and the Valley of Beit Shean**
   The Jordan Valley and its settlements; Beit Shean; Ein Harod; the mosaics of Beit Alpha; Crusader Belvoir and the kibbutzim of the Upper Jordan Valley   90-95

V **Northward from Jerusalem** — to Nebi Samuel and new neighbourhoods close by; biblical Gibeon; Ramallah; Shiloh; Samaria; Megiddo; Nazareth and Mount Tabor   96-109

VI **Around the Sea of Galilee**
   Tiberias; Ancient Hammath Tiberias; Tabgha; The Mount of Beatitudes; Capernaum; Korazin; Kibbutz Ein Gev; Susita and Byzantine Kursi   110-121

VII **Upper Galilee and the Golan**
   Safed; Meron; Kibbutz Ayelet Ha'Shahar; Tel Hatzor; the Huleh; Horshat Tal; Metullah (and the Good Fence); Banias; Castle Nimrod and Hammath Gader   122-131

VIII **Westward from Jerusalem** — through the Jerusalem Corridor to Kiryat Anavim; Abu Ghosh; Bab el-Wad; the Monastery of Latrun; Beit Shemesh with its stalactite cave; Tel Gezer; Ramle; Lydda and Rehovot.   132-137

IX **The Coast Road from Lebanon to Egypt**
   Rosh Ha'Nikra; Nahariya; Acre; Haifa; the Bahai Temple; Elijah's Altar; Beit Shearim; Daliyat el-Carmel and the Druze; Caesarea; Natanya; Herzlia; Tel Aviv-Jaffa; Ashdod; Ashkelon and Gaza; Yamit   138-149

X **South from Beersheba to Elath**
   Sde Boker; Avdat, Shivta, Mamshit and the Nabateans; Hatzeva; Yotvata; Timna; Elath   150-157
   The Seven Species   158
   Flowers of Israel   159
   People of Israel   160
   Notes   161-165
   Chronological Table   166
   Index   167-168

"The Lord made a covenant with Abram, saying, unto thy seed have I given this land, from the river of Egypt unto the Great River."

Genesis 15:18.

THE LAND OF ISRAEL IS THE REALIZATION OF A DREAM. Promised by God to Abraham and his descendants; the heritage to which the children of Israel were led by Moses after the Exodus from Egypt; welded into a powerful Hebrew nation under David and Solomon; the birthplace of Jesus and the cradle of the three great monotheistic religions, Israel is famed throughout the world as the wellspring of the Bible.

From the beginning of recorded time Israel, sometimes called Palestine, has been a coveted prize. Its fertility and strategic position attracted first the Canaanite tribes who displaced the earliest agriculturalists some 5,000 years ago, then the Hebrews, who united the country to form a strong kingdom about 1000 BCE.

Standing across the lines of communication between the great empires, Palestine was often overrun, and Assyria, Egypt, Babylon, Greece, Rome and Byzantia in turn assumed control. Then came the Crusaders, the Mamelukes, the Turks and the British, but to none of them did the Holy Land have the significance it had for the Jews, bound to Eretz Israel by a deep, single-minded devotion.

Despite these upheavals and the ever-changing waves of invaders, Jews never abandoned the hope of returning to their ancient home. Since the Roman destruction of the Second Temple 2,000 years back there has always been a larger or smaller Jewish presence in the Promised Land, while the believing Jew prays daily for the Lord to "Gather our disper-

Israel, view from a satellite

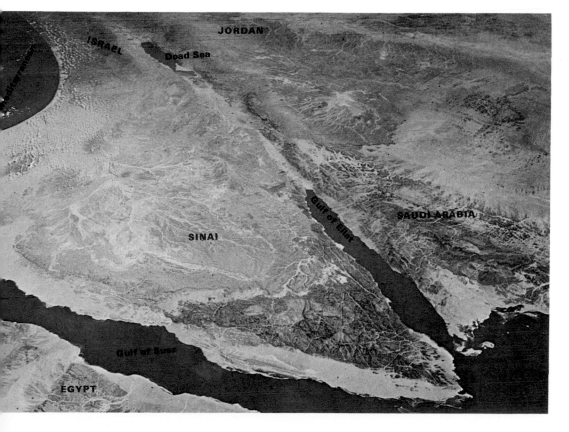

sions from among the nations, assemble our outcasts from the ends of the earth, conduct us unto Zion, thy city, with joyful song, and unto Jerusalem, the residence of thy holy temple, with everlasting joy."

Thus the continual recollection of Jewish nationhood and a specific homeland kept green the memory of over a thousand years of self-rule, and provided a favourable climate for the past century's rising tide of Zionist consciousness. Budding anew in the mind of Theodore Herzl, it was climaxed on 15th May 1948 by the proclamation of the State of Israel — the only instance in the history of mankind where a small nation, crushed and scattered, succeeded in re-establishing itself as a sovereign realm.

Israel's Colourful Past.

No book can compare with the Bible as a guide to the history and geography of the Holy Land. Open your Bible, and you will read how, nearly 4,000 years ago, Abraham, with his wife Sarah, his household, his flocks and herds, journeyed southward from Mesopotamia to the Land of Canaan, where the Canaanite tribes had lived for centuries under a loosely-knit system of city states.

One of these states was Salem, or Jerusalem, and Genesis 14:18 tells how "Melchizedek king of Salem brought forth bread and wine... and said, Blessed be Abram of the most high God," warmly welcoming the patriarch Abraham and all his company. Strange it is that, even in those far-off days, before the Jewish faith was codified, only Jerusalem's kings added "zedek," or "righteous", to their names.

The Bible goes on to relate the story of Abraham's descendants and the family mausoleum still to be seen in Hebron; of the Exodus, until to-day celebrated in every Jewish home during Passover; of Joshua crossing the River Jordan, and of his many conquests, including those of Jericho, Hatzor and Megiddo.

Next, the period of the Judges is vividly described, with Samson playing a dramatic role in the Philistine cities of Gaza, Ashdod and Ashkelon, and the prophet Samuel anointing Saul king over all Israel. Incidentally, the remains of Saul's palace are yet visible at Tel el Ful, on the outskirts of Jerusalem — the capital city to which David brought the Holy Ark, initiating an era of power and glory under David himself and his son, Solomon.

Rehoboam "forsook the counsel of the old men... that stood before Solomon his father," (I Kings 12:8) and faced a revolt resulting in the secession of the north into a separate kingdom, Israel, while Rehoboam remained ruler of Judah, with Jerusalem as its capital. Israel survived until 721 BCE, and Judah until 586 BCE, when it fell to Babylon.

Within fifty years, encouraged by a benevolent Persian regime, many Jews returned to Zion under the leadership of Ezra and Nehemiah, and a new temple arose on the ruins of the first. Palestine was absorbed into the Persian Empire, which was conquered by Alexander the Great in 332 BCE. At first benign, Greek rule later became so oppressive that the Jews rebelled. Led by the Maccabean family — Mattathias and his five sons — independence was achieved in 165 BCE and the sacred altar re-dedicated, an event commemorated on Chanukah, or the Feast of Lights.

The Hasmonean, or Maccabean, dynasty governed well for a hundred years, but in 63 BCE two young princes of the royal line brought in Pompey, a Roman general then in Syria, to mediate between them on who should ascend the throne. Seizing the opportunity, Rome stepped in and soon set up a puppet king, Herod the Edomite, nominally a Jew — a man whose abnormal personality expressed itself in a lust for power, extreme cruelty and a mania for building. He rebuilt Jerusalem and the Temple, and among his other constructions were Caesarea, Samaria and Masada on the Dead Sea. After Herod's death in 4 BCE, Palestine came under undisputed Roman rule, and it was this era which saw Jesus' trial and execution — an event with repercussions still echoing down the ages.

Jesus' prophecy that in Jerusalem the enemy "shall not leave one stone upon another," (Luke 19:44) came to pass in 70 CE, when Roman general, Titus, razed Jerusalem and the Temple. Of the Jews who managed to escape, some set up centres of learning at Yavne, on the coast, while others, like the brave defenders of Masada on the shores of the Dead Sea and Gamla in the Golan, held out for another three years. One further bid for freedom was made in 132 CE by Simon bar Kochba, who kindled a flame of independence which burned for three years, when the Jewish zealot forces were cruelly massacred.

As Roman power declined, that of Byzantia grew, particularly when Christianity was adopted as the official religion of the Empire by Constantine and his mother, Queen Helena. In 326 CE Helena visited Jerusalem and erected churches and chapels above sacred sites, such as the Church of the Holy Sepulchre, the Eleona on the Mount of Olives, the Church of the Nativity in Bethlehem, and the basilica at Abraham's Oak near Hebron, initiating a period of material prosperity in a well-tended, flourishing Palestine.

Suddenly, a veritable whirlwind arose from the small pagan town of Mecca in Saudi Arabia, where Muhammed, a young Arab, proclaimed a new religion — Islam — based on the monotheistic teachings of the Hebrew prophets. Muhammed mobilized troops to force conversion to Islam. By 634 CE the Byzantine army south of the Sea of Galilee was crushed, and within a few years Palestine was overrun. Until 1099 it remained under Moslem domination, then the Crusaders stormed in from the sea and captured Jerusalem in one of the bloodiest battles in recorded history.

The Twelve Tribes

The Crusaders lost their last foothold in the Holy Land when Acre fell in 1291, and until 1516, when Palestine became part of the Turkish Empire, it was at the mercy of the Mameluke invaders. Turkish sovereignty, too, was largely a story of neglect and indifference under which the country

7

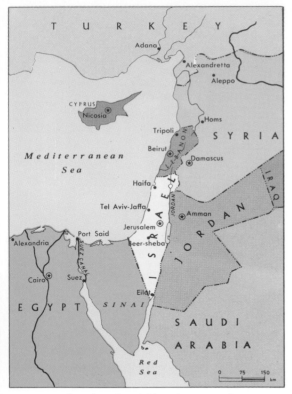

Israel and neighbouring countries

suffered for 400 years, but as Turkish authority weakened, Jewish people began to make their way in greater and greater numbers to the homeland of their prayers.

Zionism became a force to be reckoned with. In 1897 Herzl founded the World Zionist Organization and sponsored the first Zionist Congress, and when World War I broke out almost 85,000 Jews lived in Palestine. They welcomed the Balfour Declaration of 1917 for the creation of a Jewish National Home in Palestine, and enthusiastically received General Allenby when, in December of the same year, he led Britain's victorious warriors. They welcomed, too, the 1922 decision to grant Britain the mandate over Palestine, but their expectations were unfulfilled.

The rising Nazism of the 1930's, and the subsequent European holocaust, combined with British restriction of refugee immigration to what should have been a haven for the homeless, embittered British-Arab-Jewish relations. Feelings ran high; unrest and continual friction came to a head with the establishment of the Jewish State, but thousands of precious lives were to be lost before it became a reality.

Since then, surrounded as it is by Arab countries, Israel has had to fight for its existence. 1956 saw the Sinai campaign, aimed to prevent the constant incursion of infiltrators who attacked peaceful villages and tried to disrupt daily life. In 1967 came the Six Day War, then the War of Attrition, a war of snipers and skirmishes, then the Day of Atonement War of 1973. Israel's casualties since 1948 have been nearly 5000 killed and three times that number wounded. The price of independence is often high.

However, the future has begun to look brighter. In November 1977, President Anwar Sadat visited Prime Minister Menachem Begin in Jerusalem, and so began their historic peace mission. The peace treaty with Egypt was signed in Washington under the auspices of President Jimmy Carter, in March 1979. Since then, there have been many changes. President Ronald Reagan replaced President Carter in January 1981, and in October 1981 Sadat was murdered President Husni Mubarak, his successor, is continuing along the same lines, and normalization of relations between Egypt and Israel is progressing. In April 1982 the final transfer of Sinai to the Egyptians was made, but plans are in hand for two-way tourism and other contacts.

The Land and its Salient Features.

Israel's shore-line is the eastern seaboard of the Mediterranean, and its territory extends northwards through the Golan heights and southwards through the Negev to the Sinai peninsula. To the north is Lebanon, northeast is Syria, east is Jordan, while Egypt lies to the south.

Before the Six Day War of 1967 Israel's area was some 8,000 square miles, and its 120 miles of sandy coast stretched from Rosh Hanikra south to Ashkelon. Israel's fertile maritime plain runs parallel to the shore, skirting the Carmel range where Elijah the prophet confronted the idol-worshippers, extends along the verdant Sharon Valley, then passes Tel Aviv to the lowlands, or Shefela — the Samson country — merging into the northern Negev. Further inland, again parallel to the coast, a range of hills descends from 4,000 feet above sea level in Upper Galilee through the uplands of Samaria, with the sacred mountain of the Samaritans, Mount Gerizim; along the Judean hills, crossing Mount Moriah, site of Solomon's Temple, and reaches the mountains of Hebron. It was along these heights that the Way of the Patriarchs ran from ancient Babylon to Egypt, with fruitful valleys to the west, and to the east, the arid desert.

The Great Rift, that extraordinary split in the earth's crust, begins beyond the sources of the River Jordan, extends southward through the Sea of Galilee and the Jordan Valley, and continues to the Dead Sea — the lowest spot in the world, 1290 feet below sea level. From this mineral-rich lake, the rift runs south again through the Arava into the Red Sea, then for many hundreds of miles deep into Eastern Africa.

A Word on Israel's Climate.

For about eight months of the year Israel revels in warm and sunny weather. Winter rains fall between December and March, sometimes even in April, usually in storms of two or three days duration , with bright, mild intervals. It is difficult to state the average annual rainfall, for there are great variations, with northern Israel enjoying over 32 inches of rain each year, while the amount decreases as you travel south until in Elath it is barely 1 inch.

Water and water conservation is of the utmost importance in Israel, and the Israeli looks to the rains to fill the reservoirs and underwater lakes as well as the cisterns, and provide all-the-year-round supplies for agricultural, industrial and domestic use.

Israel's Varied Scenery.

Perhaps the most attractive aspect of Israel is its infinite variety: from the lush vegetation of the Galilee with its abundance of flowers, through the fields and orchards of the Shefela, to the sandy Negev and bleak mountains and rock-strewn wadis of Sinai, where Moses heard the voice of God and received the Ten Commandments.

		Tiassic-Jurassic mainly marine
Neogene-Quaternary		Paleo-Mesozoic sediments mainly continental sandstones (Nubian)
Paleogene mainly marine carbonates		Messo-Cenozoic igneous (mainly basic vocanic)
Upper Cretaceous marine		Precambrian, mainly acid intrusives

Simplified Geological Map of Israel

Deer and gazelles can be found both in the desert wastes and in the wooded hills; a few wild boar and water buffalo still roam around the remnants of the Huleh swamp, and many smaller creatures people the woodlands, pastures and river beds. Hundreds of species of birds nest in or migrate through Israel, their sweet songs and happy chirping forming a soothing background everywhere except in the heart of town.

Israel's Population and Population Structure.

Population-wise, too, variations are great. Of Israel's just over 4 million people, 3.33 million are Jews, some 525,000 Moslems, 95,000 are Christians, mainly Christian Arabs, and 53,000 are Druze, mostly living in Upper Galilee. Ten thousand Karaites considered as full Jews, have settled around Ramle and Lod, in the lowlands; 500 of the ancient faith of the Samaritans are divided between Nablus (Shechem) and Holon near Tel Aviv, while there are two small communities of Circassians, one at Rihaniya and the other at Kfar Kana.

Counted among the Moslems are around 44.000 Bedouin nomads, many still dwelling in goat-skin tents in the Negev, as the Patriarchs did four thousand years back. After the Six Day War, an additional million Arabs came under Israel's jurisdiction, with 400.000 inhabitants in Gaza and over 700.000 in Judea and Samaria. East Jerusalem's 75,000 souls were immediately absorbed into Greater Jerusalem.

When the Jewish State came into being in 1948, about 750,000 Jews lived there, who automatically became Israeli citizens. Most were of European descent, well-trained, well-educated, and with at least some experience in politics and statehood. When the gates were opened, almost a million immigrants flooded in, often without skills or possessions, straining the untried resources of the infant organization.

At that time few came from the west — instead they streamed in from Arab countries where poverty, disease and ignorance were rife. It was a modern miracle that this challenge was met, and the newcomers were settled, trained and cared for. Today, nearly half of the 3.33 million Jews are "Sabras," or native born, while of the remainder, half hail from Europe and America, and half from Asia and Africa. From a hundred different lands they came home, bringing with them the special arts, dress, customs and culture that together weave the multi-hued tapestry of Israel.

A Brief Look at Education in its Wider Sense (and allied Functions).

Hebrew — the language of the Old Testament — is the language of Israel. English and Arabic are also studied, while in Arab schools the language of instruction is Arabic. Primary education between the ages of 6 and 15 is free and compulsory, and illiteracy is very low. Among the Arab population, too, with the improvement in the educational system, illiteracy has dropped considerably.

After Primary School, there is a choice of Secondary School or a Vocational Training Centre, depending on the ability of the child and other circumstances. Religious-trend schools, where special stress is laid on Biblical and Talmudic studies, are also available, and there are countless Yeshivot ranging from orthodox to super-orthodox in their outlook.

Higher education is on an international standard with the Hebrew University in Jerusalem, Universities in Tel Aviv, Haifa and Beersheba, the Bar Ilan religious-trend university, the Weizman Institute in Rehovot and the Haifa Technion being known the world over. The army, too, in which boys serve for three years — from 18 to 21 — and girls for two, is a great educator and leveller.

Israel has forged ahead in industry, commerce and agriculture. Its principle exports are cut diamonds, citrus, agricultural and fruit products and fashion goods, while others include electrical and electronic equipment, plastics, chemicals and fertilizers, eggs, flowers and out-of-season vegetables.

On the cultural scene, too, the Israel Philharmonic Orchestra, of world repute, was founded in pre-state Palestine. Other orchestras, theatre and dance companies are making amazing progress, as well as the film-making groups. Archaeology and other arts and sciences are forging ahead, and the Israel Museum, the Tel Aviv Museum and Museum Ha'aretz are but symbols of the urge to learn and to impart knowledge. Two other flourishing fields are those of book production and philately. Israel's Philatelic Services and high-quality stamps are well known as are the Stamp Exhibitions, while the Jerusalem International Book Fair is second only to that of Frankfurt.

One all-important aspect of Israel must not be overlooked — the fact that it is the only country in the world which observes the biblical precept, "Six days shalt thou labor, and do all thy work: but the seventh day is the Sabbath of the Lord." (Exodus 20:9-10). Saturday is the official day of rest. Offices, banks, shops and schools close and most transport stops with the advent of the Sabbath; Jewish religious holidays are honoured, and Israel's minorities are encouraged to keep up their own festivals. Synagogues and places of worship are filled to overflowing, and in most areas a Sabbath calm reigns.

Far more could be written, but seeing will certainly give you a better picture of Israel and its people, so with this short glimpse at the country's background and history, let us start out on the unforgettable experience of a journey through the Holy Land.

Antique Map of the Holy Land

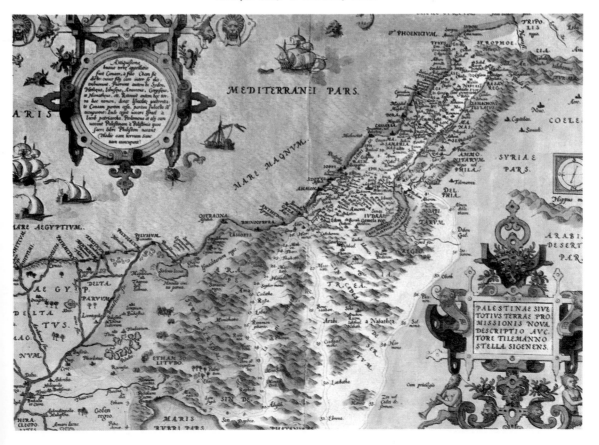

SHALOM שלום

SOME FACTS ABOUT ISRAEL

Regime: Democratic. Elections to the Knesset, which has 120 members, are held every four years. The Knesset chooses the government. The President of the State is elected by the Knesset, and his duties are largely formal.

COMMUNICATIONS AND POSTAL SERVICES

Telecommunications exist between Israel and most parts of the world. There is a direct dialling system to many countries.

Public telephones are operated by special tokens, which are available at post offices and kiosks.

Telegrams can be sent from post offices and by telephone (tel. 171).

Post offices are open weekdays from 8-12.30 and 15.45-18.00. Wednesday 8-14.00.

DISTANCES (in kilometres)

	Jerusalem	Tel-Aviv	Haifa	Tiberias	Nablus	Beer Sheba
Jerusalem	xxx	61	151	161	59	81
Tel-Aviv	61	xxx	95	126	57	105
Haifa	151	95	xxx	69	93	208
Tiberias	161	126	69	xxx	102	234
Nablus	59	57	93	102	xxx	140
Beer Sheba	81	105	208	234	140	xxx
Eilat	309	346	449	414	369	241
Ashkelon	73	52	156	181	109	64
Hadera	100	45	51	84	55	157
Metulla	225	190	118	64	166	298
Sdom	124	187	290	229	174	82
Safed	197	162	72	36	138	270

MEASUREMENTS mile = 1,6 kilometres; foot = 33 cms; yard = 96 cms. inch = 2.5 cms; pound = 454 gms; acre = 4 dunam.

NEWSPAPERS, T.V. AND RADIO

All European weeklies are available in Israel. Dailies from abroad arrive one or two days later.

In Israel, newspapers are published daily, weekly or monthly in every language.

Israel television broadcasting for adults begins at 6.30p.m. and finishes around midnight. There is only one channel. Most televisions in Israel have good reception of Jordan, which also broadcasts programmes in English.

The Israel radio broadcasts the news in English at 7.00, 13.00, 18.00 and 20.00 daily. There is good reception of the B.B.C.

INTERURBAN TRAVEL

Bus services generally start at 5 a.m. and main routes run until 11.30 p.m. On Fridays and holiday eves, public transport stops about an hour before Sabbath or the holiday.

Rail travel is also possible between certain centres. Sherut (shared taxis) follow fixed interurban routes and carry 7 passengers.

Temperatures are also different:

cent.	fahr.
0	32
15	59
20	68
25	77
26	79
27	81
28	82
29	84
30	86
31	88

cent.	fahr.
32	90
33	91
34	93
35	95
36	97
38	100
39	102
40	104

DIETARY LAWS AND SABBATH

The kosher kitchen is based on two main principles — firstly, only meat permitted by the Torah and slaughtered by a licensed "shochet" (ritual slaughterer) may be eaten, and secondly, there is complete separation between meat and milk.

Not all restaurants in Israel observe Kashrut. Kosher restaurants are checked regularly by supervisors appointed by the Rabbinate. You can ask the restaurant proprietor to show you his certificate. Most hotels are kosher, so don't be put out if you are not offered coffee with milk after a meat meal.

The Sabbath (Shabbat) commences on Friday at sunset and terminates 25 hours later. All government offices and public institutions are closed. There is no public transport in most towns, but taxis and sherut work non-stop. Offices, cinemas and theatres are also closed as are many restaurants.

However, you can always find gas stations and restaurants which will be pleased to serve you also on the Sabbath.

SAY IT IN IVRIT AND ARABIC
EVERY DAY VOCABULARY

	Ivrit	Arabic
Hello	— Shalom	— Marchaba
Goodbye	— Shalom	— Ma es-Salaameh
Thank you	— Toda	— Shukran
Excuse me	— Slicha	— Ismach Li
Please	— Bevakasha	— T'fadal
Yes	— Ken	— Aiwa
No	— Lo	Lah
Where	— Eifo	— Wain
How much?	— Kama?	— Adesh
Large	— Gadol	— Kabir
Small	— Katan	— Z'rir
Cheap	— Zol	— R'cheas
Expensive	— Yakar	— Rali
Nice	— Yafeh	— Chilu

SOME WORDS FOR TOURING

Scenery	— Nof	— Manthar
Road	— Kvish	— Sikeh
Street	— Rechov	— Sharea
Guide	— Madrich	— Murshed
Bathroom	— Sheirutim	— Chadmat
Tent	— Ohell	— Chemeh
Hotel	— Malon	— Otel
Hills	— Harim	— J'bal
Valley	— Emek	— Wadi
Information	— Modiin	— Istachbariat
River	— Nahar	— Naher
Car	— Mechonit	— Sayarah
Right	— Yemin	— Yamin
Left	— Smol	— Smal

PHRASES & EXPRESSIONS

I am a tourist	— Ani tayar	— Ana Tayar
It doesn't matter	— Ein davar	— Ma'alesh
Fine	— Beseder	— Tayeb
I have	— Yesh li	— Indi
I don't have	— Ein li	— Ma Indi
How much does it cost?	— Kama ze oleh?	— Adesh Hatha
Pleased to meet you	— Naim meod	— Hanian Judan
The time please?	— Ma ha sha'a?	— Adesh i-Seah
Leave it to me	— S'moch alay	— Orken Alay
It will be all right	— Yiye tov!	— Bissir Cher

SHOPPING GUIDE
— What's worth buying and how!

Many tourists buy fur coats and leather garments in Israel. There is a large choice of these, and prices are very reasonable.

Works of art are also greatly in demand by tourists. People from all over the world have settled in Israel, bringing with them many different skills, so that a large variety of artistic creations can be found, also at moderate prices.

Jewellery, diamonds, precious stones and silver, gold and olivewood articles are also popular with tourists. These can be found to suit every taste and every pocket.

Of course, Israel is the Holy Land, so it is natural that it should be a centre for religious articles and holy books.

What else is worth buying in Israel? Wines, antiquities — but only with a certificate proving that they are authentic, ceramics, embroidery, glassware and other decorative handmade objects. And anything else that may take your fancy...

In certain shops and especially in Arab markets, you can bargain. It is simply considered part of business. Try it once — even if you don't manage to lower the price, you will at least have had a truly oriental experience!

The exchange rate in Israel changes daily. It usually rises, which means that each day your dollar, sterling or franc is worth more in Israeli currency. You will find the exchange rate in every bank and newspaper. Shops are generally open between 8.30 — 13.00 and 16.00 — 19.00. On Fridays and holiday eves, they close at 14.00.

Banks are open daily from 8.30—12.00 and 16.00 — 17.30. Wednesdays and Fridays 8.30 — 12.00.

Mens' Shirts

American	British	Israeli/European
14½	14½	37
15	15	38
15½	15½	39
16	16	41
16½	16½	42
17	17	43

Ladies' Shoes

American	British	Israeli/European
5	3½	36
6	4½	37
7	5½	39
8	6½	40
9	7½	41
10	8½	43

Mens' Shoes

American	British	Israeli/European
8	7½	42
9	8½	43
10	9½	44
11	10½	46
12	11½	47
13	12½	48

Dresses, Knitwear, Underwear

American	British	Israeli/European
8	10	34
10	12	36/38
12	14	40
14	16	42
16	18	44/46
18	20	48

Sweaters and Pullovers

American	British	Israeli/European
32	34	40
34	36	42
36	38	44
38	40	46
40	42	48
42	44	50
44	46	52

Mens' Suits and Coats

British/American	Israeli/European
36	46
38	48
40	50
42	52
44	54
46	56

Jerusalem, by David Roberts (1839)

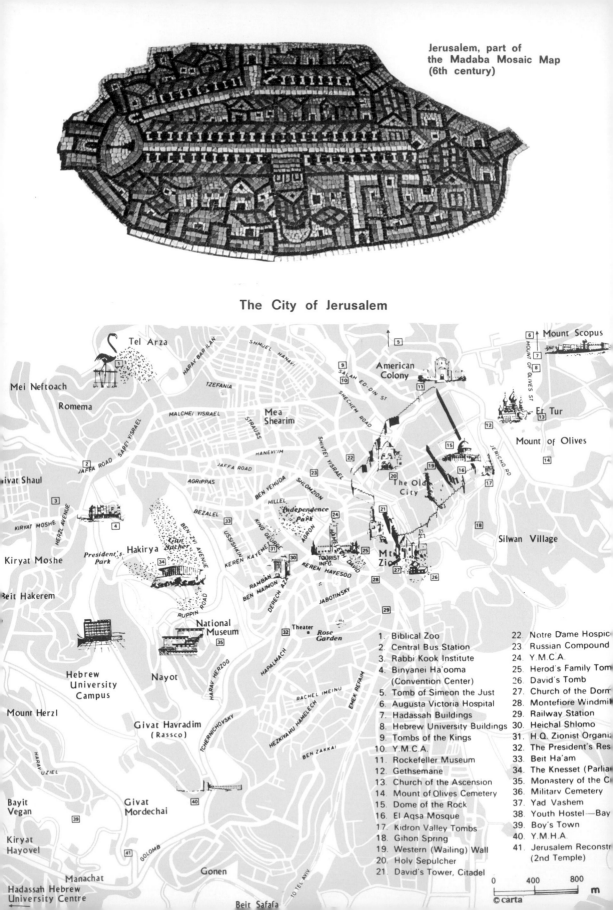

Jerusalem, part of
the Madaba Mosaic Map
(6th century)

The City of Jerusalem

1. Biblical Zoo
2. Central Bus Station
3. Rabbi Kook Institute
4. Binyanei Ha'ooma
   (Convention Center)
5. Tomb of Simeon the Just
6. Augusta Victoria Hospital
7. Hadassah Buildings
8. Hebrew University Buildings
9. Tombs of the Kings
10. Y.M.C.A.
11. Rockefeller Museum
12. Gethsemane
13. Church of the Ascension
14. Mount of Olives Cemetery
15. Dome of the Rock
16. El Aqsa Mosque
17. Kidron Valley Tombs
18. Gihon Spring
19. Western (Wailing) Wall
20. Holy Sepulcher
21. David's Tower, Citadel

22. Notre Dame Hospic
23. Russian Compound
24. Y.M.C.A.
25. Herod's Family Tom
26. David's Tomb
27. Church of the Dorm
28. Montefiore Windmil
29. Railway Station
30. Heichal Shlomo
31. H.Q. Zionist Organiza
32. The President's Res
33. Beit Ha'am
34. The Knesset (Parliam
35. Monastery of the C
36. Military Cemetery
37. Yad Vashem
38. Youth Hostel—Bay
39. Boy's Town
40. Y.M.H.A.
41. Jerusalem Reconstr
    (2nd Temple)

0   400   800 m

©carta

"Thus saith the Lord God; this is Jerusalem: I have set it in the midst of the nations."

Ezekiel 5:5.

FIVE THOUSAND YEARS of constant habitation, together with its biblical associations, have made Jerusalem unique. Situated on the watershed between the Mediterranean and the Dead Sea, and on the ancient Way of the Patriarchs linking the northern empires to Egypt in the south, it has from time immemorial been an important junction — a meeting-place not only of roads but of cultures from the north, south, east and west.

Jerusalem itself lies on a triangular plateau about 2,500 feet above sea level, creating a pass through the 3,000 feet high Hebron-Beth'el range. The Temple Mount, or Mount Moriah, is its northern edge, and two smaller hills — Mount Zion on the west and Mount Ophel on the east — separated by the Tyropoeon Valley, form the south-pointing apex.

Because of its proximity to the Gihon Spring, the only fresh-water source in the vicinity, the Canaanites established one of their city-states on narrow Mount Ophel nearly 5000 years ago.

Here Abraham met King Melchizedek, "priest of the most high God," (Genesis 14:18), and here was the stronghold of Zion, which in 1000 BCE was captured by David and transformed into the political and religious capital of the Jews — a position held for over a millenium, temporarily lost, then regained.

For fifty shekels of silver David bought the threshing floor of Araunah the Jebusite just north of Mount Ophel "to build an altar unto the Lord." (II Samuel 24:21). Above this altar Solomon erected the First Temple, and turned Jerusalem into a centre of pilgrimage, thus implementing the injunction in Deuteronomy 16:16, that "Three times a year shall all thy males appear before the Lord... in the feast of unleavened bread, in the feast of weeks and in the feast of tabernacles."

Milestones in Jerusalem's long history were the Babylonian conquest of 586 BCE; the Return to Zion and rebuilding of the Temple fifty years later; the accession of the Hasmonean and Herodian dynasties; Jesus' life, trial and crucifixion by the Roman authorities, and the razing of the Second Temple in 70 CE.

Simon bar Kochba's unsuccessful rising, quashed in 135 CE, diminished but did not extinguish Jewish presence in the Holy City, to which three centuries of Byzantine rule added a new, Christian-oriented dimension.

The sixth century CE Madaba Mosaic map, discovered in Jordan in 1896 shows its colonnaded streets and fine churches, some unearthed in recent excavations. The year 638 CE saw the Moslem invasion; 1099 that of the Crusaders who were ousted from Jerusalem by Saladin in 1187, and 1516 that of the Turks, who marched in and took over the city.

During these long years of Jerusalem's partial eclipse, Jews were always there in greater or smaller numbers, depending on local conditions and those abroad. The Spanish Inquisition, for example, forced many Jews to flee from Spain, and a number made their homes in Jerusalem. Further immigration followed. Colonies were founded, and Zionism became an active movement, progressing to the Balfour Declaration of 1917, the British Mandate over Palestine in 1920, and the 1948 Declaration of Independence.

June 1967 brought about the re-unification of Jerusalem which had been divided in 1948, the Old City and East Jerusalem coming under Jordanian rule, while West Jerusalem remained Jewish. Today, re-united Jerusalem — Israel's eternal capital — is prospering. Its population of approximately 407,000, composed of 290,000 Jews, about 90.000 Moslem and Christian Arabs, and the rest Christians of various denominations live amicably together. Multi-storied buildings jostle ancient monumental tombs; modern electric cables and water carriers lie alongside First and Second Temple aqueducts, and six-lane highways cross the footpaths trodden by biblical prophets, while Jerusalem's ramparts rise majestically above the bustle of everyday life.

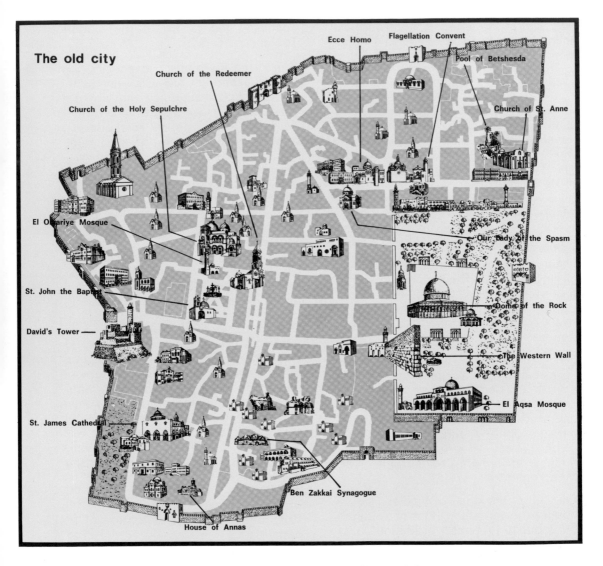

The old city

Ecce Homo
Flagellation Convent
Pool of Betshesda
Church of the Redeemer
Church of St. Anne
Church of the Holy Sepulchre
El Omariye Mosque
Our Lady of the Spasm
St. John the Baptist
Dome of the Rock
David's Tower
The Western Wall
St. James Cathedral
El Aqsa Mosque
Ben Zakkai Synagogue
House of Annas

Jerusalem, view from the Mount of Olives

"Pray for the peace of Jerusalem: They shall prosper that love thee. Peace be within thy walls, and prosperity within thy palaces".
                                                                    Psalm 122:6-7.

Jerusalem, the Citadel (David's Tower)

Part of the Model of Jerusalem
19 Cent. by Stefan Ilies

THE CITY WALLS, constructed of great blocks of grey stone, are basically those built by Turkish sultan Suleiman between 1536 and 1539, on the foundations of Roman Aelia Capitolina. Measuring 2½ miles in circumference and varying from 30 to 60 feet in height according to the conformation of the land, the walls are pierced by **four main gates.** Jaffa Gate lies on the west; Damascus Gate, or Sha'ar Shechem on the north, the Lions' Gate, also called St. Stephen's the east, and Zion Gate on the south. Others are the New Gate and Herod's Gate or the Gate of the Lady Mary on into the Christian Quarter and the second into the Moslem Quarter; the blocked Golden Gate on the east, and the Dung Gate, opening on to the Western Wall. on the south.

Adjoining Jaffa Gate is the **Citadel of Jerusalem,** once the fortress guarding Herod the Great's palace. One of the original towers, the Tower of Phasael, named for Herod's brother, still remains for it was incorporated into the battlements when the Crusaders, then the Mamelukes, rebuilt this strategic bastion. Within the courtyard, excavations revealed parts of the Hasmonean city wall of 100 BCE and pottery from the time of the First Monarchy. Incidentally, the popular term "The Tower of David" is applied sometimes to the Phasael Tower and sometimes to the fourteenth century minaret at the further end of the compound.

Golden Gate or Gate of Mercy

Jaffa Gate

"Our feet shall stand within thy gates, O Jerusalem. Jerusalem is

Damascus Gate

The D

Zion Gate   The New Gate

ilded as a city that is compact together" (Psalm 122, 2-3)

e   St. Stephen's Gate or Lions' Gate   Herod's Gate.

The Old City Wall, Jaffa Gate and the Citadel

King Solomon's Quarries

Solomon's Quarries burrow deep into the ground under the Moslem Quarter of the Old City. From these caverns Herod's masons quarried the rocks for the renewal of the Temple.

Unfounded legends tell that, in 586 BCE, King Zedekiah fled through these subterranean corridors to Jericho.

Four quarters — the Jewish Quarter in the south-east; the Armenian Quarter in the south-west; the Christian Quarter in the north-west, and the Moslem Quarter in the north-east — make up the **Old City of Jerusalem.**

The areas are defined by two stepped, cobbled streets, one running north to south from the Damascus to the Zion Gate, and the other due east from Jaffa Gate to the Temple Mount.

The Dome of the Rock (Mosque of Omar)

The Temple Mount, although geographically divided between the Jewish and the Moslem Quarters, is spiritually part of the Jewish heritage. Called Mount Moriah, or Haram el-Sharif — the Enclosure of the Noble Sanctuary — it is traditionally the place where "the Lord God formed man of the dust of the ground," (Genesis 2:7), and where Abraham bound Isaac for sacrifice. Here on the hillcrest, was David's altar, over which Solomon built the Temple, eventually to be replaced by Herod's magnificent structure, of which the Western Wall still stands.

Laid waste by the Romans, who set their pagan images upon the sacred shrine of the Jews, the Temple Mount was abandoned during Byzantine times. When Caliph Omar entered Jerusalem in 638 CE, he found the hilltop refuse-strewn and desolate. As this same spot was considered to be the scene of Mohammed's miraculous night journey, and the holiest shrine of Islam after Mecca and Medina, he cleansed the place and put up a simple wooden mosque there.

Later, Damascus-based Caliph Abd el-Malik, anxious to build up his prestige against a rival caliph who governed Mecca and Medina, erected the Dome of the Rock on the same site. Completed in 691, this golden-crowned mosque, looking much as it does now, became the centre of Moslem worship and, except for the period of Crusader domination in Jerusalem (1099 to 1187) it has remained so ever since. Other landmarks on the Temple Mount are silver-domed el-Aqsa, built in 710 on the traditional site of Solomon's Palace and the Palace of the Kings of Judah, and the tiny Dome of the Chain, said to have been used as a treasury.

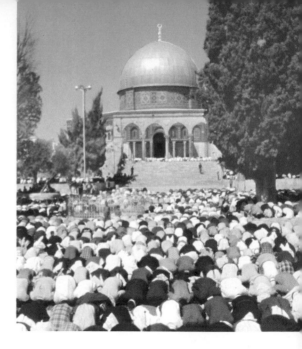

The Temple Mount

Moslems praying in the yard of the Dome of the Rock

1. Antonia Fortress	6. Suleiman's Dome	11. Dome of the Rock	16. El Kas Fountain
2. Dome of Solomon	7. Throne of Solomon	12. Dome of the Chain	17. Mograbi Gate
3. Bab el-Atem	8. The Golden Gate	13. Sun dial	18. El Aqsa Mosque
4. Bab Hutta	9. Dome of the Spirits	14. Summer Pulpit	19. Islamic Museum
5. Bab el-Asbat	10. Dome of Ascension	15. Dome of Moses	20. Solomon's Stables

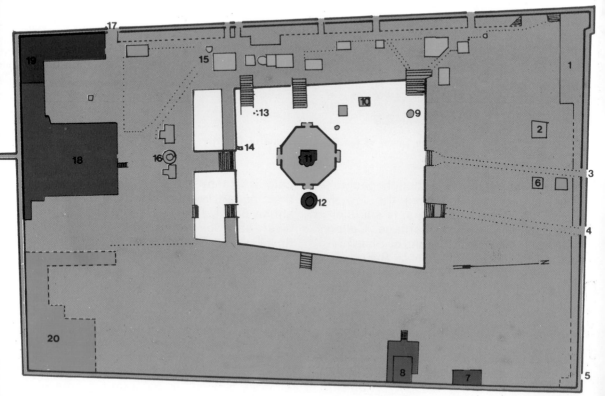

Moslem washing feet before entering Mosque Removing shoes   Reading the Koran

The interior of the Dome of the Rock

The El-Aqsa Mosque

Silver-domed **el-Aqsa Mosque** was built in 710 CE along the southern edge of the Temple precincts, on the traditional site of Solomon's Palace and the Palace of the early kings of Judah. Its seven-arched portico gives on to a dignified prayer hall, with a mihrab, or Moslem praying niche, on its south wall set, as is the custom, towards Mecca.

Steps to the east of el-Aqsa, in the paved courtyard, lead down to the subterranean vaults called Solomon's Stables. Between el-Aqsa and the Dome of the Rock is a round fountain — el Kas, or the Cup — where Moslems wash their feet and hands before worship.

The Western Wall, a section of the 2000-year-old retaining wall of Herod's Temple, is the symbol of Jewry's unwavering faith and devotion. Since 70 CE it has been the focus of Jewish pilgrimage, substituting for the Tem-

Solomon's Stables

ple pilgrimages of happier days, for even after Rome's harsh edicts of banishment, Jews were allowed to pray there on the Ninth of Av — anniversary of the Temple's destruction. Only during the 19 years of Jordanian occupation, from 1948 to 1967, were Jews forbidden to approach the hallowed site.

Huge Herodian ashlars from the original construction make up twelve courses of stones, each nearly 1½ metres in height, while above are signs of Mameluke and Turkish renovations. Exploring the vaults and aqueducts beneath Wilson's Viaduct, north of the exposed wall, you can look down into the pier cut by Sir Charles Warren in 1867, which reveals another 18 courses, reaching down to bedrock. This awe-inspiring structure, however, is not merely an imposing monument. Its spiritual content is felt by the pro-

fusion of tear-stained petitions tucked into the crannies between the blocks; by countless legends of the Holy Spirit that hovers over the Western Wall, and by the multitudes of Jews who, bringing their hopes and fears, their aspirations and their thanksgiving, come to pay homage at the Western Wall.

Professor Binyamin Mazar's **archaeological dig** along the southern edge of Mount Moriah, which began in 1968, draws a vivid picture of daily life in and around the Temple precincts when it was at the height of its glory. Among the many finds were a 40 feet wide paved road skirting the Temple area; a stairway 300 feet in width ascending to the Hulda Gates; stone vessels, some for holding sacrifices; a coping-stone marked as the place from where the priests blew the ritual trumpet, and an inscription, "When you see this

Wilson's Arch

The Western Wall and the Dome of the Rock background: the Hebrew University Campus on Mt. Scopus

The inscription discovered on one of the stones of the Western Wall during the 1969 excavations. The inscription reads: "And when ye see this, your heart shall rejoice and your bones (shall flourish) like an herb" (Isaiah 66, 14)

your heart shall rejoice and your bones shall flourish like an herb." (Isaiah 66: 14). Regal Byzantine buildings and palaces of the Ummayad period were also unearthed.
Excavations in the Jewish Quarter, directed by Professor Nahman Avigad,

have broadened the canvas of Jewish life in Jerusalem during the Second Temple era to include that of contemporary patriarchal families. Elegantly furnished mansions came to light under the debris and the thick layer of ashes resulting from the burning of

Praying at the Western Wall

Excavated ascent to the Temple Mount

The Southern and Western Wall excavations. In the centre are the remains of Robinson's Arch,

the town by the Romans. An unexpected discovery was that of a section of the city wall dating back to the seventh century BCE.

Particularly interesting are the recently restored **Spanish synagogues** in the Jewish Quarter. Clustered together into a single compound, they were built in the early sixteenth century by Jewish refugees from Spain, and have since been in almost continual use. Earliest of the synagogues in the Quarter and now being restored is the Karaite synagogue, said to date from 767 CE; then comes that of Rabbi Moses ben Nahman from 1267, while nearby are the ruins of the nineteenth century Hurva. Tiferet Israel, or the Nissan Bak synagogue, is also still in ruins, for these and dozens of other synagogues, Yeshivot and religious schools were looted and wrecked during the Jordanian occupation.

Inscription "To the Place of Trumpeting... to herald," uncovered below the northwestern parapet of the Western Wall. From here, a priest would proclaim the advent and end of the Sabbath.

Coin from the Bar-Kochba revolt against Rome (132-135 C.E.). One side of the coin depicts the Second Temple, built by Herod, with the Ark of the Covenant inside and the name Simon. The other side shows a lulav and ethrog and the inscription "For the liberation of Jerusalem".

The Jewish Quarter has been born anew. Conforming to the traditional style of former building, beautiful homes, with courtyards and patios, have been constructed, as well as large Yeshivot and other centres of learning. One of the foci in the Quarter revolves round the Batei Machseh courtyard where temporary homes were provided for Jewish immigrants.

Here is the Yeshivat Hakotel, where the foundations of the gigantic sixth century "Nea" basilica were discovered, here is the Rothschild House, bearing the Rothschild arms and motto, and here were buried the victims of the 1948 siege.

An interesting site in the heart of the Quarter is the mediaeval St. Mary of the Teutons, a complex of a church, a hospital and a hostel, now transformed into an Archaeological Garden.

The Jewish Quarter of the Old City

The Cardo in the Old City

Synagogues in the Old City

A walk along the Via Dolorosa is a "must." Traditionally the path followed by Jesus from the Judgement Court to Golgotha, it begins at the Lion's Gate and winds through to the Church of the Holy Sepulchre, touching all the fourteen Stations of the Cross. Places to see en route are the Crusader Church of St. Anne, with the Pool of Bethesda in its grounds; the First Station, once Herod's Antonia fortress, where Pontius Pilate sentenced Jesus to death, and the Ecce Homo Arch from which Pilate is supposed to have pointed at Jesus and proclaimed, "Behold the man!"

Via Dolorosa

The Via Dolorosa

The Stations of the Cross are as follows:

Stn. I	Antonia Fortress: Pilate condemns Jesus.
Stn. II	Lithostrotos: Jesus receives the Cross.
Stn. III	Jesus falls under the weight of the Cross.
Stn. IV	Mary sees Jesus with the Cross.
Stn. V	Simon of Cyrene is made to take the Cross.
Stn. VI	Veronica wipes Jesus' face.
Stn. VII	Jesus falls a second time.
Stn. VIII	Jesus speaks to the women of Jerusalem.
Stn. IX	Jesus falls a third time.
Stn. X	Calvary: Jesus is stripped of his garments.
Stn. XI	Calvary: Jesus is nailed to the Cross.
Stn. XII	Calvary: Jesus dies on the Cross.
Stn. XIII	Calvary: Jesus' body is taken from the Cross.
Stn. XIV	Holy Sepulchre: Jesus' body is laid in the Tomb of Joseph of Arimathea.

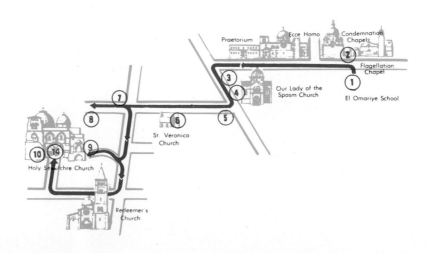

The Ecce Homo Arch, in fact, dates from at least a hundred years after Pilate's time, for it is part of a triumphal gateway erected in 135 CE as the eastern entry into Aelia Capitolina, a segment of which is incorporated into the convent chapel of the Sisters of Zion. The convent, standing on the paved courtyard of the Antonia fortress, called the Lithostrotos, is well worth visiting, and so is the Chapel of Flagellation.

Stations ten to fourteen are within the **Church of the Holy Sepulchre,** or the Church of the Resurrection, originally built by Emperor Constantine and his mother Helena in 335 CE. Cutting away the rock around Jesus' tomb to make it free-standing, Constantine then enclosed it in a separate round building — the Rotunda — and added a spacious basilica to the east. Destroyed by the Persians in 614, and again by mad Caliph Hakim in 1009,

The Lithostrotos

The Church of the Holy Sepulchre

it was rebuilt by the Crusaders in the form in which it appears to-day. The pillared Rotunda; Golgotha; the Greek Choir and the underground Chapel of the Cross deserve special attention.

Entering through the main door, you notice a slab of polished red marble — the Stone of the Anointing. On the right are the steps up to the mound **Golgotha,** with the 10th, 11th, 12th and 13th Stations of the Cross, said to mark the place Jesus was stripped of his garments, nailed to the cross, died, and was taken for burial. Station 14, the Tomb of Jesus is enclosed within the pillared Rotunda, where a small anteroom, known as the Chapel of the Angels, opens into the sepulchre.

Extending east from the Rotunda is the elongated Greek Choir or Catholikon, while to the west, behind the sepulchre, are rock-hewn Seond Temple burial loculi, indicating the site of a Jewish cemetery of those times. Beneath Golgotha, a wide stairway

Calvary, in the Church of the Holy Sepulchre

descends to **St. Helena's Grotto,** formerly the crypt of the original fourth century basilica of Constantine the Great. In the furthermost corner of the Grotto is the traditional **Cave of the Finding of the Cross,** where, it is said, relics of the cross were discovered.

The Armenian Quarter is the home of several thousand Armenians, a closely-knit people whose national home is Armenia in the USSR, while their spiritual home is here. Attached to Jeru-salem since 300 CE, when they adopted the Christian religion a generation before it was accepted by Constantine, the Armenian Compound contains the historic Cathedral and Monastery of St. James, the Armenian Patriarchate, schools and a theological seminary, a printing press, two libraries, one of rare Armenian manuscripts, and a Museum housed in the former Seminary.

Today a large Theological Seminary is rising on the site of Herod's

Palace and the Palace of the Crusader Kings, and a new church is being built on the remains of the traditional Armenian House of Caiaphas. A little known sidelight on Armenian history is that descendants of Herod the Great and Mariamne became kings of Armenia in the first century CE.

Jerusalem's markets display an unusually broad range of products. Perhaps most fascinating are the oriental vaulted markets of the Old City, for here can be seen coloured Hebron glass, handwoven rugs and embroidered dresses; straw baskets of every shape and size; ebony and wood inlaid with mother-of-pearl; leather goods; both folkcraft and expensive jewellery, and countless other items. Everyday shopping — grocery, nuts and spices — can be done there, too, while the stacks of luscious fruit and vegetables piled up in the halls of the Crusader Hospital of St. John are only equalled by those in West Jerusalem's Mahane Yehuda. Smaller markets can be found in many districts, among the most colourful being those in the Bukharin Quarter and in Mea Shearim, where you can also find a number of antique and silver shops concentrating on Jewish ritual accessories.

Jerusalem Market Scenes

Mount Zion

Mount Zion outside the Armenian Quarter carries on it the Dormition Abbey, sanctified as the place of Mary's death, and the traditional Coenaculum, or Cenacle, the Hall of the Last Supper — the "large upper room furnished and prepared," (Mark 14:15), where Jesus sat with his disciples at the Passover Seder table. Below the Cenacle is what is known as the "Hall of the Washing of the Feet," where Jesus is believed to have poured "water into a basin, and began to wash the disciples' feet." (John 13:5). Leading off the hall is a chamber with an enormous cenotaph, which folklore holds to be King David's Tomb. Still highly revered, during the occupation years from 1948 to 1967, it acted as a substitute for the unapproachable Western Wall.

King David's Tomb

The Room of the Last Supper

St. Peter in Gallicantu, with ancient Maccabean stairway on the right

St. Peter in Gallicantu stands on the generally accepted House of Caiaphas, High Priest at the time of Jesus' execution. Here Peter is said to have denied his master, according to Jesus' prophecy that, "Before the cock crow, thou shalt deny me thrice." (Luke 22: 61). A Maccabean stairway, connecting Mount Zion to the Gihon Spring, can still be seen, and excavations have revealed inscriptions and weights and measures of Second Temple times, as well as a rock-cut flagellation post.
Mount Ophel, the more easterly of Jerusalem's two southern hills, is the site of David's City and of the Tombs of the Kings of Judah. Excavations there brought to light part of the Jebusite ramparts of 4000 years ago, Israelite houses and fortifications of 3000 years back, as well as later walls and towers. Many smaller items were found, outstanding among them being a Greek-inscribed stone tablet from a synagogue of the early first century CE.

The Site of the City of David —
new excavations

XV XII

1. Titus from Mount Scopus

Women's gate

Third wall   Simon Gioras

Our sanctuary is laid broken down, our templ[e]

tower

Camp of Tenth Legion

N E W   Q U A R T E R

Alexander's tomb

Assyrian camp

Second camp

Second wall

Siege dike

2. Tenth Legio[n] from Jericho

Markets

5 ▼

XII

7

Antonia

9

4

S E C O N D
Q U A R T E R

10

3. Breaching of wall

5

Temple

11. Destruction of Temple

8. Daily sacrifices ceased

Hyrcanus' tomb

XV

Amygdalon pool

Phasaelis

Hippicus

Simon Gioras

Temple court

Herod's palace

Miriamme

14

13

Camp

13

U P P E R
C I T Y

12

...d's family tomb

...on
...es

Pool of Siloam

K i d r o n   V a l l e y

Siege dike

Simon Gioras

6. Construction of siege-wall

Pompey's camp

Siege dike

Ananias' tomb

V a l l e y   o f
t h e   s p r i n g

0   50   100   150 yards
0   50   100 meters

Map of the siege of Jerusalem, showing all the sections of Jerusalem at the time of the Second Temple. The topographical situation of Jerusalem, lying on two hills and surrounded by valleys, is also shown.

In biblical days the Gihon Spring was Jerusalem's only water supply, and when enemies were at the gate, first priority was the safety of the spring. The second book of Chronicles, 32:30, tells how King "Hezekiah stopped the upper watercourse of Gihon, and brought it straight down to the west side of the city of David." This extraordinary conduit, now known as the **Silwan Tunnel**, was dug around 700 BCE to bring water directly into the town and is still being used. An inscription in ancient Hebrew script found chiselled into the conduit wall, commemorates the meeting of Hezekiah's two work gangs who began at each end of the tunnel and met midway. Here, at the biblical city of David, a major archaeological dig is going on, and remarkable finds have been made.

Along the **Kidron Valley,** which runs between Mount Ophel and the Mount of Olives, are a row of Second Temple monumental sepulchres — the Pillar of Absalom; the Tomb of Jehoshaphat; the Pyramid of Zachariah and the Mausoleum of Bnei Hezir, a priestly family mentioned in I Chronicles 24:15. Sometimes called the Valley of Jehoshaphat, sometimes Wadi en-Nar — the Valley of Fire — it continues through steep rock scarps to the Dead Sea.

Hezekiah's Tunnel

The Siloam Inscription

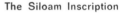

The Pool of Siloam

| Absalom's Pillar | Tomb of Bnei Hezir (St. James' Tomb) | Zachariah's Tomb |

Tombs in the Kidron Valley

Olivet, or the **Mount of Olives,** has from biblical days held a special meaning for the Jewish people. King David "went up by the ascent of mount Olivet," (II Samuel 15:30), while legends tell that the Messiah will enter the Temple Courts through the now-blocked Golden Gate opposite the mountain. For this reason, pious Jews have, for untold generations, chosen the Mount of Olives as a burial place, to be among the first to follow the Messiah on the Day of Redemption.

Christians, too, venerate Olivet for its associations with Jesus' last days on earth, and the mountain abounds in Christian shrines. One of them is the **Church of the Assumption,** built above a majestic stairway descending to the crypt where Mary was buried, and then taken up to heaven.

The eastern wall of the Old City, the Golden Gate and golden Dome of the Rock, viewed from the Garden of Gethsemane

The Basilica of the Agony

Adjoining is the **Grotto of Gethsemane,** a shallow cave where Israelite farmers prepared olive oil thousands of years ago — a cave in which Jesus and his companions often sheltered from winter rain and summer sunshine.

An oil press is called in Hebrew "gat shemen," and from this stemmed the world "Gethsemane."

Close by are the ancient olive trees of the Garden of Gethsemane surrounding the **Basilica of the Agony,** its blue and gold mosaic pediment visible from afar. Also known as the Church of All Nations, for it was sponsored jointly by several countries, it was erected by the Italian church architect, Antonio Barluzzi, over the remains of two earlier churches, one from Byzantine and one from Crusader times.

Another Barluzzi gem, one of his last assignments before his death, is the Franciscan chapel of **Dominus Flevit,** where Jesus is said to have wept as

The Church of All Nations with the Church of Mary Magdalene in the background

Panoramic view of the Mount of Olives showing the sk Hotel and in the centre, the white Dome of Ascensio

he foresaw the doom of Jerusalem. Entirely different is the White Russian onion-turreted **Church of Mary Magdalene,** built by Czar Alexander III in memory of his mother.

Higher up is the **Eleona,** or the Paternoster Church, originally erected in the fourth century by Empress Helena, mother of Constantine. A cavern where Jesus taught his disciples the Lord's Prayer is now a chapel, and the Carmelite cloister here is lined with glazed tiles bearing the text of the prayer translated into 44 languages.

The soaring **Ascension Tower** of the White Russian nuns, called e-Tur, quite overshadows the **Chapel of Ascension,** a tiny edicule with finely carved Crusader capitals roofing a rock impressed with Jesus' last earthly footprint. This is the traditionally accepted site of Jesus' ascent to heaven. A round shrine built over the spot in 380 was partially destroyed by the Persians in 614. It was later reconstructed by the Crusaders, who built a polygonal chapel open to the sky and enclosed by an octagonal wall. In 1187, the shrine was taken by the Moslems and the central chapel covered by a cupola. The Chapel of the Ascension was the main architectural inspiration for the Dome of the Rock.

In the grounds, look out for a small cave revered by Jews, Christians and Moslems alike. Jews link it with the **Grave of Hulda,** the biblical prophetess, Christians believe that a fifth century saint, Pelagia, lived there,

Paternoster

the whole City of Jerusalem, with the Old City of Jerusalem in the background. To the left is the Intercontinental

Ancient olive trees in the Garden of Gethsemane   The Tomb of the Virgin Mary

Dominus Flevit and a view of the Old City

while Moslems claim it was the home of Rabieh el-Adawiyah, a holy woman of the eighth century. Before leaving the Mount of Olives. take note of the curious circular catacomb — the Tomb of the Prophets — where Haggai, Malachi and Zachariah are said to have been interred, and over which rises the modern Intercontinental Hotel.

Before going up to Mount Scopus note the Rockefeller Museum; the American Colony, founded a hundred years ago by Chicago lawyer, Horatio Spafford, and the magnificent **Tomb of the Kings.** The Tomb of the Kings comprises a majestic rock-hewn stairway down to the funerary court and sepulchres of the royal family of Adiabene. At the turn of the Christian era, Queen Helena of Adiabene and her son, Prince Izates, converted to Judaism, settled in Jerusalem, and came to the help of the Jews against the Romans.

Note, too, the housing development of French Hill and Ramat Eshkol — their broad avenues, excellent shopping centres and other facilities, and comfortable apartments and houses have arisen on what was waste land before 1967. On Mount Scopus itself the outstanding features are Hadassah's rebuilt, modernized hospital, the

The Dome of Ascension

Hebrew University with its many innovations and spacious amphitheatre overlooking the Dead Sea and, on the outskirts of the Uni-

The Tomb of the Kings

The interior of the Dome of Ascension

45

versity, the Augusta Victoria Hospital. Built in 1910, it was the residence of the British Governor-General from the end of World War I until 1927. Its square pointed tower is a Jerusalem landmark.

Mount Scopus, the northern extension of Olivet, is one of the most strategic heights around Jerusalem. Josephus Flavius writes how Roman general Gallus "pitched his camp on Scopus," (Wars 2:19:4), then Titus, and afterwards the Crusaders, also stationed their troops there. In recent history, too, Scopus played a fateful role, for in 1948 the Israelis, who remained in possession of the Hebrew University and Hadassah Hospital, held on to Scopus, but the road link with the rest of Jerusalem was cut. When the Six Day War broke out, connection was immediately made and the road to Scopus re-taken. Since then, the Hebrew University campus has been magnificently rebuilt, and it is today one of the finest and most modern universities the world over.

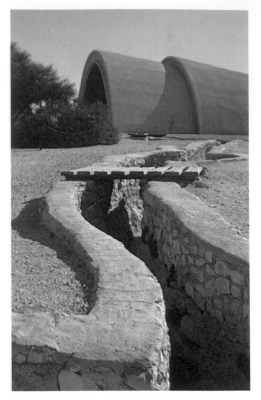

Memorial site on Ammunition Hill

Aerial view of the Hadassah Medical Centre on Mount Scopus

THE TOMB

THEN TOOK THEY THE BODY OF JESUS, AND WOUND IT IN LINEN CLOTHES WITH THE SPICES, AS THE MANNER OF THE JEWS IS TO BURY. NOW IN THE PLACE WHERE HE WAS CRUCIFIED THERE WAS A GARDEN; AND IN THE GARDEN A NEW SEPULCHRE, WHEREIN WAS NEVER MAN YET LAID.

THERE LAID THEY JESUS THEREFORE BECAUSE OF THE JEWS' PREPARATION DAY; FOR THE SEPULCHRE WAS NIGH AT HAND.

John 19: 40-42

ויקחו את גופת ישוע ויעטוה בתכריכים אשר מלאו בשמים כדרך קבורת היהודים:
ובמקום אשר נצלב שם היה גן ובו קבר חדש אשר עוד לא נקבר בו א׳ש: ובהיות
היום ערב שבת ליהודים והקבר קרוב קברו בו את ישוע:

יוחנן 19: 40-42

ΤΟ ΜΝΗΜΕΙΟΝ

ΕΛΑΒΟΝ ΟΥΝ ΤΟ ΣΩΜΑ ΤΟΥ ΙΗΣΟΥ ΚΑΙ ΕΔΗΣΑΝ ΑΥΤΟ ΟΘΟΝΙΟΙΣ ΜΕΤΑ ΤΩΝ ΑΡΩΜΑΤΩΝ, ΚΑΘΩΣ ΕΘΟΣ ΕΣΤΙ ΤΟΙΣ ΙΟΥΔΑΙΟΙΣ ΕΝΤΑΦΙΑΖΕΙΝ. ΗΝ ΔΕ ΕΝ ΤΩ ΤΟΠΩ ΟΠΟΥ ΕΣΤΑΥΡΩΘΗ ΚΗΠΟΣ, ΚΑΙ ΕΝ ΤΩ ΚΗΠΩ ΜΝΗΜΕΙΟΝ ΚΑΙΝΟΝ, ΕΝ Ω ΟΥΔΕΠΩ ΟΥΔΕΙΣ ΕΤΕΘΗ. ΕΚΕΙ ΟΥΝ ΔΙΑ ΤΗΝ ΠΑΡΑΣΚΕΥΗΝ ΤΩΝ ΙΟΥΔΑΙΩΝ, ΟΤΙ ΕΓΓΥΣ ΗΝ ΤΟ ΜΝΗΜΕΙΟΝ, ΕΘΗΚΑΝ ΤΟΝ ΙΗΣΟΥΝ.

Ιωάννης 19: 40-42

Not everyone believes that the Church of the Holy Sepulchre is truly the grave of Jesus. Many non-Catholic sects hold that it is actually in the **Garden Tomb,** set in a quiet enclosure just outside the Damascus Gate.

These sites have become publicised in recent years because — apart from any archaeological significance — they provide visitors with a visual aid to the Gospel story of the death and resurrection of Jesus.

In 1882 the British General Gordon was a leading advocate for the area near Damascus Gate as a probable site of the crucifixion.

Jewish and Christian traditions associate the ground with the "Place of Stoning" and the sepulchre nearby, which Dame Kathleen Kenyon has described as a 'first century tomb', was purchased in 1893 by the Garden Tomb Association with H.Q. in London.

The New Testament declares that 'In the place where Jesus was crucified there was a garden and in the Garden a new Tomb' (John 19:41).

The evidence for a probable site of execution near to an exceptionally large cistern (which indicates the possibility of a Vineyard Garden) and

Gordon's Calvary

a Herodian tomb which meets all the details mentioned in the New Testament makes the present garden a meaningful centre for Christian meditation and devotion.

The Sepulchre and Weeping Chamber

The Old City Wall and Citadel at night

"Awake, awake, put on thy strength, o Zion; put on thy beautiful garments, o Jerusalem, the holy city."   *Isaiah 52:1*

Mishkenot Sha'ananim

NEW JERUSALEM is essentially West Jerusalem outside the walls, a development which began with the construction of the row of cottages called **Mishkenot Sha'ananim** — the Dwelling-places of the Tranquil. Built in 1860 by Sir Moses Montefiore with a bequest by an American Jew, Judah Touro of New Orleans, it was intended to draw the inhabitants out of the over-crowded hovels of the Jewish Quarter of that time to a newer, healthier life. The location chosen was on the hill west of Mount Zion, across the **Valley of Hinnom,** where child sacrifice was practised in Canaanite times. At the head of the valley is the Herodian reservoir first called the Serpents' Pool, later extended by the Crusaders, when it was known as the Lake of Germanus, and then repaired by Sultan Suleiman and named Birkat Ha'-

Sultan. To-day Birkat Ha'Sultan is being transformed into a park, and Mishkenot Sha'ananim houses visiting scientists, artists, writers and musicians, while the Montefiore Windmill, once a source of employment for the tenants, is now a "Montefiore Museum."

After the first break from the confining walls of the Old City, suburbs began to mushroom, each being established by groups of people with a similar background and outlook. One of the earliest of these neighbourhoods, founded in 1874, is **Mea She'arim,** still looking much as it did a century ago. The whole community is Ashkenazi — Jews of Eastern or Central European origin — and is fanatically orthodox. Only Yiddish is spoken, for Hebrew is observed as the language of prayer. Men wear unclipped sidelocks, and dress in the long black kapote (caftan) and streimel (round felt hat) of mediaeval Poland, and the kerchiefed women are clothed in high-necked, long-sleeved dresses, while the visitor is expected to "dress modestly with head covered."

Jerusalem's **Town Centre** provides every facility for gift and other shopping, including clothes, jewellery and furs. There are few large stores — most buying is done in one-purpose shops. Restaurants are plentiful, and so are attractive cafes serving snacks and pastries. Please remember that no shops in West Jerusalem are open on the Sabbath!

There are many Sabbath services, the largest orthodox-style synagogues being the Yeshurun and Hechal Shlomo, which also houses the Chief Rabbinate. Conservative Jewry holds services very close to Hechal Shlomo, and the Reform Congregation meets in the Hebrew Union College next to the King David Hotel. While there, look across at the **West Jerusalem YMCA** with its unusual architectural style, its swimming pool, gymnasium, auditorium and small museum, and try to visit the rock-cut Herod's Family Tomb, with its perfectly preserved rolling stone.

A street scene in Mea She'arim

The Jerusalem Theatre

Partial view of West Jerusalem

Another modern architectural gem is the **Jerusalem Theatre** with its broad patios and spacious foyer. The President's Residence and the Van Leer foundation for Higher Studies are nearby, while the picturesque **Khan** — a renovated Turkish caravanserai — has regular programmes for tourists.

Jerusalem's Cultural Centre includes the Knesset building — the seat of the Israeli Parliament — built in 1966. A long, low structure of pink Jerusalem stone, with its lower floors tunnelling into the hill-side, it is closed by decorative metal gates designed by David Palombo, while in front of it stands

The Knesset (Israel's Parliament) building

The Shrine of the Book

The Knesset Menorah

Benno Elkan's menorah, carved with scenes from Jewish history. Cast in bronze, it was presented as a sign of friendship by the Parliament of Britain to that of Israel. Three magnificent tapestries by Marc Chagall, who also designed the wall and floor mosaics, hang in the large reception hall. A synagogue, reading and conference rooms, a library and a restaurant are available for the 120 Knesset members.

The buttressed walls of the mediaeval **Monastery of the Cross** enclose a sixth century Byzantine mosaic incorporated into an eleventh century church. Legends tell that here, in the Valley of the Cross, grew the tree from which the wooden Cross was made, and further, that it was Emperor Constantine himself who granted this land to the King of Georgia in the fourth century. For 1200 years Georgian monks lived and worked here in

The Habakkuk Commentary, one of the seven
Dead Sea Scrolls housed in the Shrine of the Book

The interior of the Shrine of the Book

the monastery, but eventually it was taken over by the Greek Patriarchate. Streams of people, young and old, visit the **Israel Museum,** giving it a cheerful, lively air. The many-faceted museum includes the Shrine of the Book, containing priceless biblical scrolls; a section on archaeology on an international standard; departments of Judaica and art, and the Billy Rose Sculpture Garden. Frequently changing exhibitions, activity in the Youth Wing, and a full programme of lectures and cultural films lend added interest.

The **Givat Ram campus of the Hebrew University** was planned in 1949 to replace that on Mount Scopus, inaccessible after the War of Independence. Quickly expanding, it soon trained thousands of students in the various faculties, attractively housed in buildings set among the green lawns, and gardens of the University complex. In addition to the teaching facilities, the Givat Ram campus contains the National and University Library; a large auditorium; an amphitheatre; a residential Faculty Club; a Student Cen-

The Israel Museum, Jerusalem, at night

tre with sports fields and a swimming pool, students' dormitories and an unusual synagogue. Since 1967 it has worked in conjunction with the campus on Mount Scopus.

In the grounds of the Holyland Hotel in West Jerusalem is a 1:50 scale model of **Jerusalem of the Second Tem-ple.** Built according to the measurements in Middot in the Mishnah, as well as to the description in Josephus Flavius' histories, its construction was supervised by Professor Michael Avi-Yonah. Every detail is there — the Temple itself; Herod's Palace near the Jaffa Gate; the twin-spired Palace of

The Givat Ram Campus of the Hebrew University

Model of Jerusalem at the time of the Second Temple, in the grounds of the Holyland Hotel

The Temple

the Hasmoneans: the markets, inns and ordinary dwelling houses. Not only do you see a replica of Herodian Jerusalem, but you are also able to compare it with the Old City of today. **Mount Herzl,** last resting-place of Theodor Herzl, is the highest point in West Jerusalem. It is a favourite gath-

Herzl's Tomb

The Jerusalem Military Cemetery

Yad ve'Shem Memorial

The "Ohel Yizkor" Memorial Hall

ering-spot for tourists and Israelis, especially school children, who painlessly absorb a lesson in modern history by walking around and observing the exhibits in the small Herzl Museum at the entrance.

An extension of Mount Herzl is the beautifully landscaped **Military Cemetery** for those who fell in Israel's struggle for independence and security. Here the memory of those who were lost in actions preparatory to Israel's bid for freedom is kept green, while bay trees and scented rosemary symbolize the perpetual remembrance of the victims of the 1948 War of Independence, the 1956 Sinai Campaign; the Six Day War of 1967 and the Day of Atonement War of 1973.

A third component of Mount Herzl is **Yad ve'Shem** — the memorial to the six million Jews who perished in the European holocaust. Archives and micro-films catalogue numerous documents and other evidence relating to this catastrophe, and the Hall of Remembrance, with an Eternal Light burning over human ashes from one of the crematoria, is paved with the names of the dreaded death camps.

From Mount Herzl you can see the spires and minarets of **Ein Karem,** said to be the village "in the hill country of Judah "(Luke 1:65) where John the Baptist was born. Churches, convents and monasteries abound in the picturesque valley, while around Mary's Spring, from which Mary is said to have drawn water when she visited her cousin Elisabeth, artists' galleries and a popular Music Centre have recently been opened.

General view of Ein Karem

On the hill above is the Ein Karem **Hadassah-Hebrew University Medical Centre** sponsored by Hadassah, the Women's Zionist Organization of America, with about 370,000 members. The Centre includes an 800-bed hospital; an outpatients' clinic serving more than 1000 Jews and Arabs daily; schools of medicine, dentistry, nursing and pharmacy, and the Sharett Institute, an ultra-modern cancer treatment and research institute. Hadassah takes special pride in its synagogue, adorned by Marc Chagall's series of 12 stained glass windows depicting the Twelve Sons of Jacob.

Hadassah has been based here only since 1961, although its beginnings were in 1912, when Henrietta Szold, teacher and educator, gathered together a group of 12 women who under-took to provide medical aid for neglected, backward Palestine, then still under the Turks. A team of doctors, nurses and dentists was soon on its way. Hospitals and infant care stations were opened, and schools for nursing and vocational training were set up.

In 1939 a 300-bed hospital was built on Mount Scopus in co-operation with the Hebrew University, but nine years later a 'bus carrying hospital staff to their duties was ambushed, and 78 people killed. Hadassah Hospital was then left under police guard, and the work was transferred to makeshift premises in town. After the Six Day War of 1967, Hadassah returned to Scopus and today a brand-new 300-bed Medical Centre, with every modern facility, has arisen there as an extension of the Ein Karem complex.

The Hadassah-Hebrew University Medical Centre

The Stained Glass Windows by Marc Chagall

The beautiful stained glass windows by the world-famous French Jewish artist, Marc Chagall, were presented to the synagogue of the Hadassah-Hebrew University Medical Centre in 1962 by the American Women's Hadassah Organization. They represent the sons of the Patriarch Jacob, from whom descended the twelve tribes of Israel, and their symbols. Before he died, Jacob blessed his twelve sons, describing their different characters and prophecying what would befall each of them (Genesis 49). Later, before his death, Moses also blessed the Twelve Tribes (Deut 33). The windows are painted in magnificent colours and measure about 11 feet high by 12 feet wide.

Diagram showing the location of the windows in the Synagogue

	Reuben	Simeon	Levi
Benjamin			Judah
Joseph			Zebulun
Naphtali			Issachar
	Asher	Gad	Dan

REUBEN : eldest son of Jacob, by Leah : "Thou art my firstborn, my might, and the beginning of my strength, the excellency of dignity and the excellency of power: Unstable as water, thou shalt not excel..." (Gen. 49)

SIMEON, second son of Jacob by Leah : "Simeon and Levi are brethren; instruments of cruelty are in their habitations... ...for in their anger they slew a man, and in their selfwill they digged down a wall. Cursed be their anger... I will divide them in Jacob and scatter them in Israel. (Gen. 49)

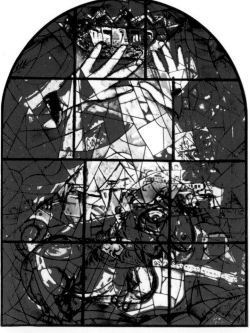

LEVI, Jacob's third son by Leah : "They shall teach Jacob thy judgements and Israel thy law : they shall put incense before thee, and whole burnt sacrifice upon thine altar. Bless ...his substance, and accept the work of his hands." (Deut. 33)

JUDAH, Jacob's fourth son by Leah : "Thou art he whom they brethren shall praise... thy father's children shall bow down before thee ...Judah is a lion's whelp... The sceptre shall not depart from Judah". (Gen. 49)

ISSACHAR, Jacob's fifth son by Leah: "Issachar is a strong ass couching between two burdens: and he saw that rest was good, and the land that it was pleasant, and bowed his shoulder to bear, and became a servant unto tribute". (Gen. 49)

ZEBULUN, Jacob's sixth son by Leah: "Zebulun shall dwell at the haven of the sea; and he shall be for an haven of ships; and his border shall be unto Zidon." (Gen. 49)

DAN, Jacob's first son by Bilhah: "Dan shall judge his people, as one of the tribes of Israel. Dan shall be a serpent by the way, an adder in the path, that biteth the horse heels, so that his rider shall fall backward". (Gen. 49)

GAD, Jacob's first son by Zilpah: "A troop shall overcome him but he shall overcome at the last." (Gen. 49)

ASHER, Jacob's second son by Zilpah: "Out of Asher shall his bread be fat, and he shall yield royal dainties" (Gen. 49). "Let Asher be blessed with children... let him dip his foot in oil... as thy days, so shall thy strength be". (Deut. 33)

NAPHTALI, Jacob's second son by Bilhah: "Naphtali is a hind let loose, he giveth goodly word" (Gen. 49). "Satisfied with favour and full with the blessing of the Lord". (Deut. 33)

JOSEPH, Jacob's first son by Rachel: "Joseph is a fruitful bough... whose branches run over the wall (Gen. 49). "His glory is like the first-ling of his bullock, and his horns are like the horns of unicorns; with them shall he push the people together to the ends of the earth". (Deut. 33)

BENJAMIN, Jacob's second son by Rachel: "Benjamin shall raven as a wolf: in the morning he shall devour the prey, and at night he shall divide the spoil". (Gen. 49)

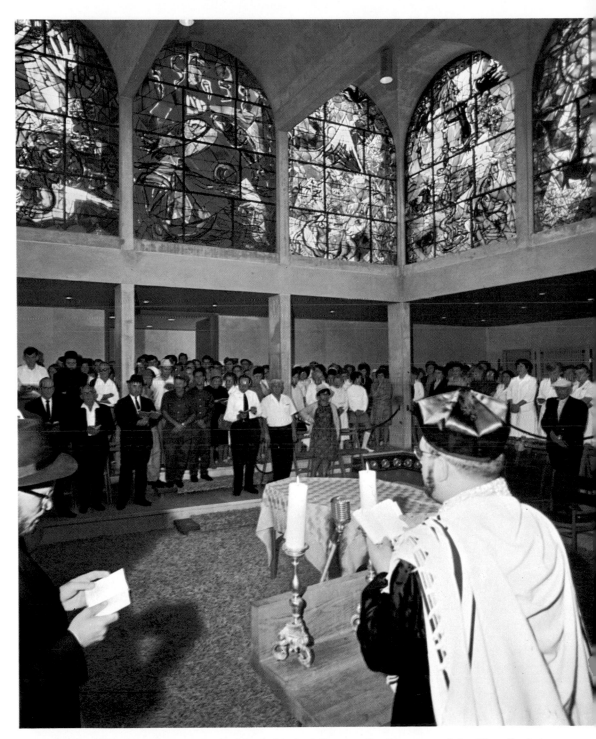

Interior of the Synagogue at the Hadassah Medical Centre, showing some of the Chagall windows

Not far away from the Ein Karem Medical Centre, set in the wooded hills around ancient Khirbet Sa'adim, is the **Kennedy Memorial.** Created in the form of a truncated tree, it symbolizes the life and violent death of John F. Kennedy, and that of his brother Robert.

The Kennedy Memorial in the Peace Forest, amidst the Judean Hills

"The Scroll of Fire", memorial to the victims of the Holocaust

Kibbutz Kiryat Anavim Guest House

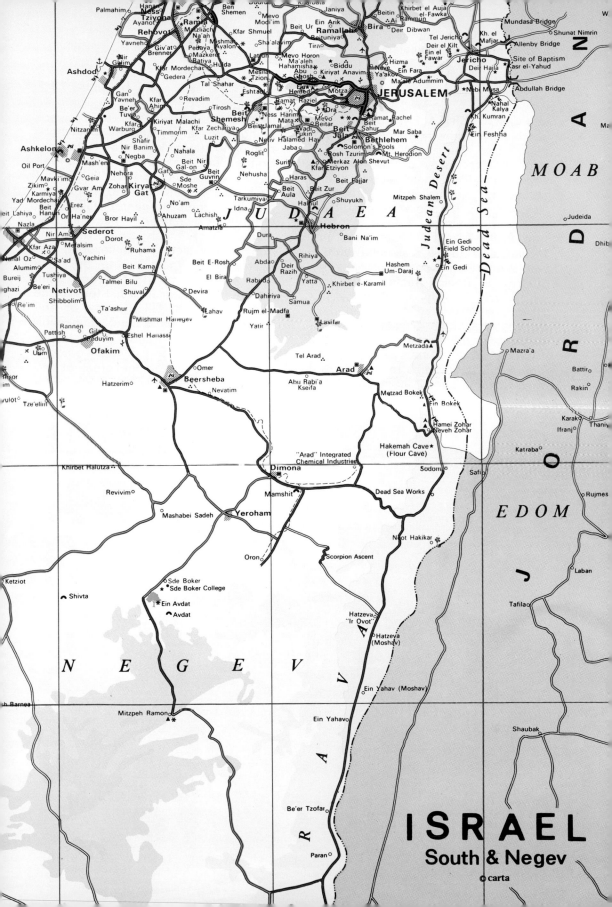

ISRAEL
South & Negev
© carta

Southward from Jerusalem

"They went out to the south of Judah, even to Beer-Sheba."

LEAVING JERUSALEM towards the south, the highway follows the ancient route along the Valley of Rephaim — the Valley of the Mists — where "the Philistines... spread themselves in the valley of Rephaim," (II Samuel 5:22) and were conquered by David. It passes **Talpiot,** not long ago on the border between Israel and Jordan, and now a residential suburb with a rapidly growing industrial zone. Nearby is **Ramat Rachel,** a kibbutz which was heavily attacked by the Egyptians during the War of Independence. After 1948 it quickly revived, expanding still further following the Six Day War, and today it also includes a guest house, a restaurant and a swimming pool. Christian folkore believes this to be the spot where Mary and Joseph rested on their journey to Bethlehem, and when

foundations for a water tower were being dug, a Byzantine commemorative monastery known as Kathisma, or the Seat, was uncovered, as well as the remains of a seventh century BCE palace from the First Monarchy. **Mar Elias,** the sixth century CE Greek Orthodox monastery, marking the place where Elijah slept when he fled from wicked Queen Jezebel, was a strategic outpost during the 1948 war. Another important strong point was the 3000 feet high hill-top village of Beit Jallah, or Giloh, home of Ahitophel, King David's chief counsellor. Today a Field School with living accommodation and a small outdoor museum, stand on the crest of the hill, replacing the guns which were trained on West Jerusalem's peaceful suburbs during the Jordanian occupation from 1948 to 1967. Rachel's

Bethlehem, with the Church of the Nativity in the centre

The Church of the Nativity

Tomb is a small domed structure marking the grave of Jacob's favourite wife, who died in childbirth and "was buried on the way to Ephrath, which is Bethlehem." (Genesis 35:19). Revered by Christians and Moslems as well as Jews, the tomb is — and has been for generations — a place of Jewish pilgrimage, where you can see throngs of pilgrims, particularly childless wives, who come to pray to the youngest and loveliest of the Matriarchs.

Mentioned as early as 333 CE by the Bordeaux Pilgrim as being covered by a pyramid of stones, it was rebuilt by the Crusaders who protected the huge cenotaph by a domed roof supported on four columns. In 1788 the arches were blocked to form a closed chamber, then in 1841 Sir Mo-

ses Montefiore repaired the building and added a vestibule with a mihrab, or south-pointing prayer niche, for Moslem worship.

Bethlehem, a friendly township of some 32,000 Christian Arabs who are skilled artisans and craftsmen, has many biblical associations reflecting a tranquil, pastoral existence. Here, nearly 4000 years back, Jacob buried his young wife Rachel; here was the home of Naomi and her family; here Ruth gleaned in the fields and met her kinsman, Boaz; here their great-grandson, David, was born, and here Samuel "anointed him in the midst of his brethren." (I Samuel 16:13).

Among Christians, Bethlehem's fame stems from Matthew 2:1, which tells that "Jesus was born in Bethlehem of Judea." Luke 2:7 goes on to des-

The Basilica of the Church of the Nativity

cribe how Mary "brought forth her firstborn son... and laid him in a manger; because there was not room in the inn." Over this cave-like manger, traditionally Jesus' birthplace, arose the **Basilica of the Nativity.**

From the very beginnings of the Christian era this was a sacred grotto, above which, in the fourth century, Emperor Constantine constructed a large church, first piercing a hole in the cave roof for the faithful to look down into the holy place, then erecting an octagonal altar over it. The altar is still there. Around two hundred years later, Emperor Justinian rebuilt the basilica much as you see it now, and put up a mosaic pediment of the Magi in Persian dress. Because of this picture, it is claimed, the ravaging Persian troops of 614 CE spared the Church of the Nativity from destruction. No basic changes were

made by the Crusaders, except for the decoration of the church with rich paintings and glass mosaics, and the addition of St. Catherine's Chapel to the north.

Approaching the Basilica of the Nativity, shared by the Armenians, the Greek Orthodox and the Latins, from the broad paved courtyard, note particularly the entrance which has been filled in below the straight, wide Byzantine lintel to outline the pointed Crusader doorway. This in turn was partially blocked by the Turks, leaving the present opening small to allow for easy defence. Crossing a covered porch you enter the rectangular prayer hall, approximately 200 by 90 feet, with four rows of twelve brown Bethlehem stone pillars; a pink marble font to the right and the original eight-sided altar directly ahead.

Curved steps descend to the Grotto, where a silver star overlies the spot of Jesus' birth. A side door opens into the secluded forecourt of the Franciscan **Chapel of St. Catherine,** sensitively restored by Antonio Barluzzi in 1933. A statue of St. Jerome, who lived here in the fifth century and translated the Bible into Latin, stands in the middle of the courtyard, while interesting crypts, said to be the burial places of St. Jerome, St. Paula and St. Eusebius of Cremona, honeycomb the rock. Another door, always kept locked, links the crypt with the Grotto of the Nativity.

Shepherds still pasture their flocks around Bethlehem, where the shepherds heard the good tidings of Jesus' birth from "the angel of the Lord." (Luke 2:9). Everywhere evidence is found of Byzantine convents and chapels with fine mosaic pavements. One, called the **Shepherds' Field,** has

The Grotto of the Nativity

The Silver Star in the Grotto of the Nativity

Rachel's Tomb

been rebuilt for the Franciscans by Antonio Barluzzi.

Close by is the village of **Tekoa,** where the prophet Amos was born, and where a Jewish settlement, formerly Nahal and now civilian, now stands. From Tekoa you can see the strange truncated cone of **Herodion,** built by Herod the Great in 37 BCE and described in detail by Josephus Flavius in his Wars of the Jews, book 1:21:10. Archaeological diggings have confirmed that in this remarkable construction Herod "built round towers all about the top, and filled the remaining space with costly palaces... He brought a mighty quantity of water from a great distance, and raised an ascent of two hundred steps of the whitest marble."

Within the enclosure are remnants of Herod's fresco-painted halls and chambers; a bath-house and one of the earliest synagogues ever discovered. Tremendous underground cis-

The Shepherds' Field, with Bethlehem in the background

terns from Herod's day have been cleared — cisterns which are now thought to have been used as the headquarters of Bar Kochba's insurrection.

Herod, Josephus writes, died in Jericho in 4 BCE and was placed on "a bier of all gold, embroidered with precious stones... and a crown of gold on his head... and the body was carried to Herodion." His grave has not yet been brought to light.

Kalat el-Burak — the Castle of the Pools — was built in Turkish times to guard the triple reservoirs called **Solomon's Pools,** from Solomon's declaration in Ecclesiastes 2:6, "I made me pools of water." Partly rock-hewn, partly masonry-built and plaster lined, these enormous artificial pools fed Herod's elaborate system of aqueducts supplying Jerusalem with water at all seasons.

Barely four miles from Solomon's

Solomon's Pools

Herodion. In the foreground : harvesting in the fields of Bethlehem, a scene reminiscent of Ruth the Moabitess who gleaned here in the fields of Boaz (Ruth 2, 3, 4, 11-13)

Pools is the religious kibbutz of **Kfar Etzion.** Founded as Migdal Edar in 1927, its members were forced to leave two years later because of Arab riots. In 1945 it was re-established and was soon joined by three other settlements. However, with the rumblings of the 1948 war, tensions rose and the situation became untenable, especially after a relief party of 35 Palmach volunteers was ambushed and wiped out in January that same year. Women and children were evacuated, but on 13th May 1948, the day before the Declaration of Independence, all defenders of Kfar Etzion were either killed or captured. However, within months of the Six Day War, the kibbutz was rehabilitated by religious youth, including children of the original pioneers. Today

Gush Etzion comprises Kfar Etzion itself, a Field School and Youth Hostel, Rosh Zurim and the urban and educational centre of Alon Shvut.

Nearing Hebron, at a place known as Mamre, you find **Ramat el-Khalil** — the Height of the Friend, as Abraham is familiarly referred to in Moslem folktales. Genesis 13:18 tells how "Abram came and dwelt in the plain of Mamre, which is in Hebron, and built there an altar to the Lord," and tradition links the site with Ramat el-Khalil. Here he is said, too, to have pitched his tent and "sat in the tent door in the heat of the day," and to have welcomed his celestial visitors, who promised Sarah that she would bear a son.

Looking at the enclosure at the present time, you see a rectangle some

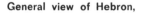

General view of Hebron,

Hebron, the Mosque of Abraham which was built over the Cave of Machpela
containing the tombs of the Patriarchs

225 by 150 feet bordered by large stones, with Abraham's Altar in the centre and Abraham's Well, still recognizable in one corner. Herod made this into an open-air temple, then it became a khan and market-place, where the pitiful remnants of Bar Kochba's army were sold into slavery. Later the Byzantine Basilica of the Terebinth was built here, and it was destroyed by the Persians in 614.

Hebron, one of Israel's four holy cities is also one of the most ancient cities, in the world, the Kiryat Arba of biblical days. Now a market town of some 50,000 Moslems, at first glance Hebron appears little different from dozens of other Arab hill towns until the majestic Cave of Machpelah — the Tomb of the Patriarchs — catches your eye. Genesis 23 relates how "Sarah died in Kirjath Arba; the same is Hebron," and how "Abraham buried Sarah his wife in the cave of Machpelah before Mamre: the same is Hebron," in the field which he bought from Ephron the Hittite for

"four hundred shekels of silver" (Genesis 23:16). Abraham himself was later buried here, and so were Isaac and Rebecca, and Jacob and Leah, while legend holds that the graves of Adam and Eve were also in the same place.

For seven years David reigned in Hebron as King of Judah, and "unto David were sons born in Hebron," (II Samuel 3:2) including handsome Absalom, who afterwards returned to Hebron and stirred up an abortive rebellion against his father. Almost a thousand years passed before Herod the Great erected the wall encircling the 150 by 90 feet compound, and paved the enclosure with great, smooth flagstones still in position. In Byzantine times it was roofed over and turned into the Church of St. Abraham, which included a special section where Jews could pray! With the Moslem invasion of 638 CE, the Church of St. Abraham became the Mosque of Abraham and, except for the interval of Crusader domination, from 1099 to 1187, it has remained so ever since. The Tomb of the Patriarchs has always been one of Jewry's most hallowed shrines, yet for centuries Jews were forbidden to ascend beyond the seventh step of the entrance staircase. Under Jordanian rule it was completely cut off, but now all pilgrims may, at specified times, enter the prayer halls with the symbolic cenotaphs set above the cave-mausoleum of the Patriarchs.

Despite the overwhelming Arab majority of recent years, Jews have always lived in Hebron, near the sepulchres of their ancestors. With the British Mandate, relations between Jews and Arabs deteriorated, culminating in 1929 with the cold-blooded massacre of peaceful citizens and Yeshiva students. Even that did not drive them out, and a number of families continued to make their homes in Hebron until 1936, when they were obliged to leave. Only from 1936 until 1967 did no Jews live in the town; then a group of orthodox young people established Kiryat Arba — a thriving urban community on the outskirts of the City of the Patriarchs.

Continuing southward through the Negev to Beersheba, the landscape becomes progressively drier and sandier. The **Negev** — its Hebrew connotation is the "dry south" — is a term encompassing most of the southern part of Israel to Eilat. Natural inhabitants of the Negev semi-desert are the nomadic **Bedouin,** wandering herdsmen, many of whom still live in tents in a manner reminiscent of the children of Israel in the Bible. Times and habits are changing. Bedouin dwellings are now often huts or houses instead of tents, and the automobile is ousting the all-purpose camel, although it is helpful not only for transport, but provides milk and cheese for food, and camel-hair for clothing and shelter.

The Tombs of Isaac and Rebecca in the Cave of Machpela

Scenes from Bedouin life ▶

The Inn of the Good Samaritan on the road to Jericho, near Maale Adumim.

mosque indicated the supposed tomb of Moses.

On this road, about midway between the two towns, there was in Second Temple times a caravanserai, the **Inn of the Good Samaritan,** scene of the story in Luke 10:30, of how a "certain man went down from Jerusalem to Jericho and fell among thieves." Robbed and injured, he was rescued by a Samaritan, who dressed his wounds and carried him to the inn. Ruins of a Turkish khan on the foundations of the Byzantine Monastery of St. Joachim mark the spot, while on the other side of the road is **Maale Adumim** — the Red Pass — where the Crusaders erected their Red Tower, a fortress protecting the pilgrim way. This strategic area is now being developed as a residential and factory district. Roads have been

Jericho, the city of date palms

laid, community facilities initiated, and hundreds of living units are being erected.

From the further side of the hill, a panorama of the Dead Sea Valley and **Jericho** and its surroundings spreads out in the shimmering heat. Jericho, thought to be one of the oldest cities in the world, swelters in the humidity of 800 feet below sea level. An abundance of water and the warm, damp air provide ideal conditions for growing exotic flowers and sub-tropical fruits like dates, bananas, mangos and papayas — indeed the main occupation of Jericho's 7000 inhabitants is agriculture.

Throughout the ages, Jericho's location has changed very little, staying close to Elisha's Spring — Ein es-Sultan — where Tel es-Sultan shows an 8000 BCE colony — the first step ever taken by man to switch from the wandering lifestyle of the herdsman to a more settled existence. Most striking is the stone-built tower, 30 feet across, with a steep internal stair rising from ground level to an opening at the top.

Excavations on the tel have taken place at irregular intervals since 1868, and early finds included the famous 9000 year old plastered skulls with shell "eyes" and white stone "teeth." Dr. Kathleen Kenyon's work of 1952 onwards revealed layer after layer of habitation until the Chalcolithic Age in the fourth millenium BCE. Some 2000 years later, activity was renewed around Elisha's Spring by the Canaanites, who built walled towns and buried their dead in shaft tombs, examples of which are displayed in the Rockefeller Museum.

One of these walled towns fell to the blast of Joshua's trumpets about 1250 BCE, and although Joshua had forbidden the rebuilding of the city, in the ninth century BCE "Hiel the Bethelite did build Jericho." (I Kings 16:34). Joshua's curse came true, for Hiel lost, or possibly sacrificed, his oldest son Abiram and his youngest son, Segub, but despite the curse, the city lasted for four hundred years.

The Maccabees used Jericho as a

Hisham's Palace, Jericho

Inscription on the 7th century mosaic floor of an ancient synagogue reading "Peace upon Israel"

Sign marking "Sea Level" on the road leading down to the Dead Sea

The Mount of Temptation seen from Tel Jericho

The Monastery of Karantel on the Mount of Temptation

district centre in the second century BCE, and the book of the Maccabees relates how Simon made Ptolemy, his Egyptian son-in-law, the local governor. Ptolemy entertained Simon and his sons, Judas and Mattathias, in the **Castle of Duk,** above Elisha's Spring when, without warning, all three were murdered in an attempt to usurp the throne. To-day, the **Monastery of Karantel,** on the Mount of Temptation, where Jesus fasted 40 days to resist the devil's offer to him of "all the kingdoms in the world," (Luke 4:5) lies below the ruins of Duk.

"Jesus entered and passed through Jericho," says Luke 19:1, but the Jericho of Jesus was not here, it was the Jericho of Herod, several miles further south. Here Herod cultivated plantations of dates, balsam, myrrh and spices, and built his winter palaces, including the Citadel of Cypros, named for his mother. In the swimming pool at Cypros, Herod drowned his popular young brother-in-law, Mariamne's brother Aristobolus, fearing he might be a serious rival to the monarchy.

In the close vicinity of Jericho exten-

sive excavations by archaeologist Ehud Netzer have revealed amazing finds, particularly from the Herodian period.

Among the places worth seeing in the vicinity is the seventh century CE synagogue floor beneath a Jericho house, bearing the Hebrew inscription, "Peace upon Israel," and the ruins of the **synagogue of Naaran,** at the fertile oasis created by the springs of Ein Duk and Ein Nueima. An aqueduct from Ein Nueima carried water to **Hisham's Palace,** or Khirbet Mafjar, the eighth century CE Winter Palace of Caliph Hisham ibn Abd el-Malik. It has a pillared courtyard; two mosques and two bath-houses with perfectly preserved mosaic floors, while in the Guest Room is an exquisite example of a mosaic carpet depicting a lion stalking three fawns nibbling at a dark-green tree. A number of the stucco decorations of human figures, animals and birds are on show in the Rockefeller Museum.

A few miles south-east of Jericho, the blue expanse of the **Dead Sea** — the lowest spot on earth, 1290 feet below sea level and three times that distance below Jerusalem — glitters in the sun. Measuring 48 miles in length, 11 miles across, and 1300 feet in depth at its deepest point, the curious oily feel of the lake water is due to the 30% of solids it contains. These are in the form of salts, the most important being magnesium, sodium, calcium and potassium chlorides, and magnesium bromide, which are refined and processed, then utilized for industrial and agricultural purposes and for export. Incidentally, the percentage of salts in the Dead Sea is over ten times that in ocean water! Travelling along the scenic western shore of the Dead Sea, or as it is called in the Bible, the Salt Sea, you soon reach **Qumran,** where heaped-up ruins at the foot of bleak, cavern-pitted cliffs aroused no particular attention until 1947, when two Bedouin shepherd boys found seven earthenware jars containing priceless biblical manuscripts. Further searches un-

Qumran, the caves where the Dead Sea Scrolls were discovered.

Qumran, ruins of the Essenes' settlement and the Dead Sea

The western shore of the Dead Sea

covered a wealth of parchment fragments and scrolls, including the unique Copper Scroll, listing the places of concealment of the Temple treasures. This scroll is in Amman, but many of the others are in Jerusalem's two main museums.

Salt formations in the Dead Sea

Floating on the Dead Sea

When the ruins were cleared in 1951, a complete Essene monastery of the second and first centuries BCE was found, including a large Assembly Hall and dining room; kitchens and laundry; a potter's kiln; cisterns; stepped ritual baths and a scriptorium. Presumably here the Essenes copied the already ancient manuscripts and hid them and the rest of their library when the Romans were at their gates. These documents remained hidden away for 2000 years.

Immediately south of Qumran, and now part of a popular bathing beach, are the fresh-water springs of **Ein Feshka.** Here the strange, semi-monastic Jewish sect of the Essenes, who studied, wrote and lived at Qumran, had their fields and pastures, and even a tannery. Here, too, was their cemetery, according to Jewish law, well away from the community's living quarters.

Mitzpeh Shalem, high above the Turba spring, is an observation post manned by Nahal — Pioneer Fighting Youth — who combine their Army service with pioneer work. About 8 miles south of Mitzpeh Shalem is the biblical oasis of Ein Gedi, where David fled from Saul "and dwelt in the strongholds at Engedi." (I Samuel 24:1).

Established in 1949 as a border kibbutz, for it was then on the edge of the Green Line between Israel and Jordan, it has developed as a kibbutz and Youth Hostel, as a Field School and as a holiday centre with an excellent Guest House. Ein David — David's Fountain — with its waterfalls and luxuriant vegetation, is a magnet for nature lovers. Added interest is stirred by the Canaanite altar on the crest of the hill; by Professor Mazar's dig revealing the perfume vats and sources of the scented "camphire in the vineyards of Engedi," (Song of Songs 1:14) and the mosaic floor of the fifth century synagogue uncovered not long ago.

Masada, where the Jews made their last desperate stand against the Romans in 73 CE, looms bleak and ominous on the skyline. Rising steeply to 1300 feet above the Dead Sea, it is topped by a broad plateau 20 acres in size, which carried Herod's magnificent constructions and where the drama of the final revolt was played out.

First fortified by the Hasmoneans as one of their line of defence bastions holding back invasion from the east, it was rebuilt by Herod as a pleasure palace. He added hanging gardens, a swimming pool, an elaborate bathhouse; vast stores; a synagogue and ritual baths, protecting the whole by sentry towers set at intervals along an encircling wall. Approach was difficult. The only way seems to have been by the narrow Snake Path, tortuously winding up the eastern slope of the mountain, from where you can

Ein Gedi, waterfall at Nachal David

Ein Gedi, Ibex in the Nature Reserve

General view of the fortress hill of Masada

Map of Masada showing the main sites of the fortress and the Roman camps

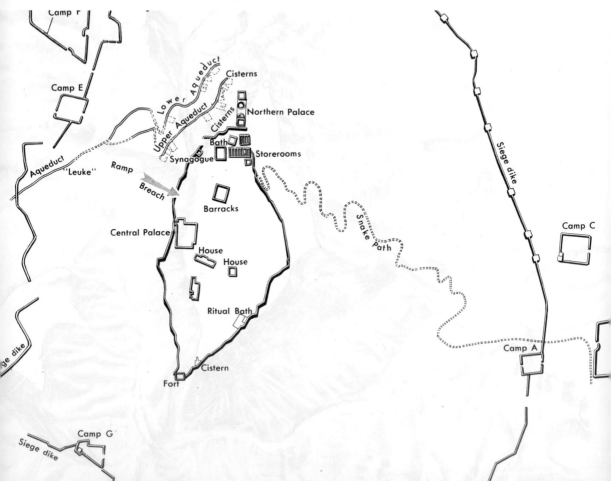

The cableway at Masada

to the defenders, enjoining each man to kill his family, then they "chose ten men by lot to slay all the rest... and when these ten had slain them all, they made the same rule for casting lots for themselves." (Wars of the Jews, book VII: 9:1). When the Romans eventually entered, they found ample stores to show it was not lack of provisions that caused their surrender; otherwise they found nothing but piles of corpses and a deathly silence.

Visiting Masada after Professor Yigael Yadin's dig and partial restoration, you can either climb the Snake Path, take the easier ascent along the Roman ramp on the west slope, or be passively lifted to the top in the cable car. On the site are the relics of

Herod's northern palace — note the three levels

see the threatening outlines of the Roman camps at the base of the hill. After the fall of Jerusalem in 70 CE, a group of 960 Jewish zealots, men, women and children, barricaded themselves on Masada and held it for three years. When conquest seemed imminent and the Romans were ready to burst in, Josephus tells that the commander, Eleazar ben Yair, spoke

Mosaic from the Herodian period

The Synagogue

The Snake Path

The Bath House

Herod's luxurious living, contrasting sharply with the simple ovens and earthenware cooking pots of the Zealots. The columbarium, possibly for the nesting of carrier pigeons for communication, and the Byzantine chapel deserve special notice, while the touching remains of the zealots last days — the lettered sherds with which the lots were cast; the crumbling parchment pages inscribed with verses from the Psalms; the tattered raiment, the sandals and the plaits of women's hair — are in the Israel Museum.

On summer evenings the tragedy is re-enacted in a sound-and-light programme telling the epic of Masada and its heroic defenders, of their last days and the final consuming fires. Nothing, however, is more moving than to be

The lower terrace of the Northern Palace

present at a ceremony on the summit of Masada, when the new recruits to the Parachute Division of Israel's Defence Army take their oath of allegiance to the State, and solemnly swear that "Masada shall not fall again!"

Radio-active hot springs have long been known to exist at **Ein Bokek.** A square Roman-Byzantine fort guarding the water source can still be seen, while modern medicine is utilizing the therapeutic value of the waters to cure, or at least alleviate, various ailments such as psoriasis, arthritis and rheumatism. A number of hotels, from five-star rating to simple accommodation have been opened at Ein Bokek, which is rapidly achieving international status as a health resort.

At the southern tip of the Dead Sea, edged by grim, grey salt rock, is **Sdom,** the accursed city of the Bible, upon which "the Lord rained... brimstone and fire," (Genesis 19:24) because of the wickedness of its people. Lot, Abraham's nephew, lived in Sdom, and before the catastrophe, he was warned to "Escape for thy life; look not behind thee." (Genesis 19: 17). However, Lot's wife did look back, "and she became a pillar of salt." (Genesis 19:26).

Present-day Sdom is very different.

"Lot's Wife" Salt Pillar, Sdom

The fortress at Zohar

Views of Arad

Salt quarries, evaporating pans and processing plants for the minerals extracted from the Dead Sea have transformed the sinful town into a hive of industry, where hard-working men skilfully prepare, pack and transport great quantities of fertilizers and chemicals for use at home and abroad.

Turning westward from Sdom through the Judean desert, you may either pass Neve Zohar and the picturesque Zohar Fortress and ascend to **Arad,** or you can pass the much-destroyed Roman Tamar Fort to reach **Dimona.** Both are successfully industrialized towns. Arad, well-planned and attractive, has a supply of natural gas, phosphate mines and a number of chemical factories. Established in 1961, its population is around 12,000, most of whom are employed in projects associated with the Dead Sea works. Other occupations are office work and teaching, as well as in the field of tourism, for Arad's dry climate and unpolluted air has made it a popular centre for curing respiratory diseases. Founded in 1955, Dimona, with nearly 30,000 inhabitants, has become an important road junction and industrial centre. Its industries are similar to those of Arad, but it has a variety of

A section of the Dead Sea Works

other factories to absorb its growing numbers, while both towns are within easy reach of Beersheba.

Sunset over the Judean Desert and the Dead Sea

The Jordan Valley and the Valley of Beit Shean

"Lot lifted up his eyes and beheld all the Plain of Jordan".

Genesis 13:10.

THE JORDAN RIVER is perhaps the most famous in the world. It is mentioned dozens of times in the Bible, and among the references are stories of how "the Lord spake unto Moses in the plains of Moab by Jordan," (Numbers 33:50), of Joshua and the children of Israel, who "passed clean over Jordan", (Joshua 3:17), and of "Jesus baptized of John in Jordan," (Mark 1:9).

From its sources, the Dan, the Hatzbani and the Banias rivulets, the Jordan winds south for about 120 miles, flowing through the Lake of Galilee and the Jordan Valley, and spilling into the northern end of the Dead Sea. Here, not far from the **Allenby** Bridge, linking Amman to Jericho, are a number of Christian shrines commemorating the Baptism of Jesus. Best known is the **Monastery of St. John** — in Arabic, Kasr el-Yahud (the Castle of the Jews) — from the tradition that here, at this shallow ford, Joshua led his people across the Jordan into the Promised Land.

Over the past few years, a remarkable engineering feat has been accomplished — the laying of a highway along the Jordan Valley from Jericho through to Beit Shean. Where a rough donkey-track once ran is a good asphalted road, making the Jordan Valley journey quick and comfortable, and connecting the new border settlements with each other and with the rest of Israel. Many of them are manned by Nahal, whose two-fold duty it is to cultivate the long-neglected soil and to protect Israel's eastern boundary.

A second road — the Allon Road — cuts through parallel to the Jordan Valley road from Maale Adumim almost to Mehola. Meant to mark the limit of settlement, it is now lined with young communities — Kochav Hashahar, Rimonim, Gitit and others, while the valley road includes Gilgal, recalling the Gilgal of Joshua 5:10,

where the children of Israel encamped and celebrated their first Passover in the Holy Land, and Phasael, after the ancient town named for Herod's brother. Masuot — in Hebrew, Beacons — is at the foot of **Sartaba,** one of the Beacon Hills of Second Temple days, from which flares were lighted to notify the scattered Jewish communities of the advent of festivals and of the New Moon. On its crest are the ruins of the Hasmonean-Herodian fortress of Alexandrion, built by Alexander Yannai. Here Herod buried his beautiful Hasmonean wife, Mariamne, her mother Alexandra, and his two sons by Mariamne, all killed on Herod's orders.

While road-breaking at **Moshav Rehov** on the outskirts of Beit Shean, a series of synagogues of the Talmudic period were unearthed. They had mosaic pavements, and on one of them was the longest Hebrew mosaic inscription ever found. It comprised 29 lines from the Jerusalem Talmud, and was unusual in that, instead of praising the donors or the craftsmen engaged in beautifying the building, it listed a large number of fruits, where

One of the bridges over the River Jordan

they were grown, and the tithes due for them.

Beit Shean, the Greek Scythopolis, was one of the great cities of olden days. An important junction from which roads fanned out north to Syria, east to Jordan, south to Egypt and west to the Mediterranean, it was at all times a supply centre for the varied produce growing in the area. Blessed with an abundance of water and fertile soil, Beit Shean has, at certain stages in its 6000-year-long history, been termed the "Gateway to Paradise".

Excavations carried out between 1929 and 1933 showed 18 levels of occupation, from the Chalcolithic era (the fourth millenium BCE) onward. Finds included Egyptian temples and several stelae inscribed with hieroglyphic writing, some of which are now in the Rockefeller Museum, Jerusalem. These and other items discovered proved that for at least three hundred years, from about the fifteenth to the twelfth centuries BCE, Beit Shean

Mosaic at the Monastery of the Lady Mary, Beit Shean

The Roman Theatre at Beit Shean

was the administrative headquarters of Egyptian rule.

Allotted to the tribe of Manasseh. there were difficulties with the local population, and Joshua 17:12 states, "the children of Manasseh could not drive out the inhabitants," although apparently they lived peaceably with the Canaanites. I Samuel 31:10 tells of Saul's death in battle with the Philistines, who "fastened his body to the wall of Beth-shean."

During the Hasmonean era many Jews lived in the city. They were massacred around 70 CE, at the end of the Roman-Jewish war, but in the Talmudic period Jews re-settled there and were active in learning and commerce. Flax was grown; linen woven and cloth manufactured, for Beit Shean was then a world centre for the textile trade and for food production. Jew and Gentile seem to have coexisted side by side, for in addition to the magnificent Roman theatre of the third century CE, remains of several large synagogues were found, including one with a Samaritan inscription. The sixth century mosaics of the **Monastery of Lady Mary** on the outskirts of Beit Shean are also well worth seeing.

The early Arab period of the seventh to the ninth centuries CE saw the continuation of Beit Shean's prosperity, and it was then famed for its dates, rice and vineyards. However, the Crusaders ruined it by taking its produce, but not cultivating the soil and allowing the water sources to run untended, creating malaria-ridden swampland. Settlement declined so drastically that, except for a temporary upsurge during the Middle Ages, about 150 years ago barely 200 souls could be found there. After World War I, under the British Mandate, Bedouin began to drift in and stayed, and they were followed by Jews from Moslem lands. The situation remained fairly stable until 1936, when all civilians left and the town became a hideout for Arab terrorists. Captured by Israeli forces in May 1948, it began to attract Jewish immigrants, and a few

The Zodiac from the mosaic floor of the ancient Synagogue at Beit Alpha

Mount Gilboa and Gan Ha'shlosha (Sakhne)

textile and other factories were opened, but Beit Shean's disadvantaged community still numbers less than 15,000.

At the foot of **Mount Gilboa** where I Samuel 31:8 describes how "they found Saul and his three sons fallen" in battle with the Philistines, are springs and pools steeped in lush vegetation. One of these well-watered spots is **Ein Harod,** where Gideon, in his fight against the Midianites, "pitched beside the well of Harod," (Judges 7:1). By these same waters Gideon, at the Lord's command, tested the men who were to accompany him to war. "The number of them that lapped, putting their hand to their mouth, were three hundred," (Judges 7:6), and these were Gideon's soldiers. Another similar place is the **Sakhne** or Gan Ha'shlosha, now a National Park, with a deep rock pool for good swimmers; shallow pools for paddlers; smooth green lawns; waterfalls and ancient water-mills.

The sixth century synagogue floor of **Beit Alpha** is one of the best examples of synagogue mosaics of this period. Accidentally discovered in 1928 when a conduit was being laid, the find was investigated and documented by Professor E.L. Sukenik. The complete ground plan revealed a rectangular area comprising an outer courtyard with a narthex, or entry porch, with three openings into the main prayer hall which has a deep, south-pointing apse — that is, pointing towards Jerusalem.

Like many similar floors, it is divided into three horizontal panels, that nearest the apse showing two menorahs and other ritual objects; the middle panel showing the Zodiac Wheel, and that nearest the entrance depicting the story of Abraham and Isaac. Just inside the central doorway is an inscription in Aramaic and Greek honouring the builders of the synagogue and giving the date as between 518 and 527.

Set on a scarp rising to 1000 feet above the Jordan Valley is **Belvoir,**

Belvoir, ruins of the Crusader fortress and the Jordan Valley

the best preserved Crusader castle in the country. Called in Arabic Kaukab el-Hawa — the Star of the Winds — and in Hebrew Kochav Ha'Yarden — the Star of the Jordan, it was one of the key fortresses of the Crusaders. In Second Temple times its name was Agrippina, one of the Beacon Hills, and during the Jewish revolt against the Romans, it was a Zealot stronghold.

Square and solid, surrounded on three sides by a moat 30 feet deep and 60 feet across, Belvoir covers an area of 32 acres. Built about 1138, it was later acquired by the Hospitallers, who held it until 1187, when Saladin besieged it. Belvoir withstood two years of siege conditions, but was forced to capitulate in 1189. When excavated in 1963, many signs of Jewish habitation were found in the vicinity, and stones engraved with Jewish symbols were seen to be incorporated in the Crusader masonry. Subsequently it was partially restored and an approach road laid, for it had been very difficult to reach except on foot or horseback. Now it is one of the National Parks, with the Castle of Belvoir as a special attraction.

Also in the Jordan Valley is **Afikim,** a kibbutz founded in 1932. Largest of the kibbutzim, with about 1350 members, it has effectively combined agriculture with industry on a large scale. Afikim's plywood factory particularly has become widely known, and it produces enough plywood and allied items to supply local needs as well as the export market. Adjacent is Kibbutz **Shaar Ha'Golan,** with an excellent museum of local prehistory.

Degania, "Mother of the Collective Villages," was started as a pioneer project in 1909 at the outlet of the Jordan from Lake Kinneret. Conditions at the time were almost unbearable — the hot, humid climate, disease, unfamiliarity with the land, and marauding Arab bands, combined to discourage the would-be farmers, most of whom came from Europe. Despite all setbacks, the Jewish colonists were determined to remain, and their unflinching heroism paved the way to a good future. Today Degania, the fore-runner of many comparable settlements, is flourishing. Together with its sister community, Degania B, its 1000 members live happily among the field gardens and orchards that they themselves created. The term **"Kibbutz"** needs a little explanation. It signifies a communal settlement, mainly agricultural, in which, according to the official definition "there is no private wealth and which is responsible for all the needs of the members and their families." From the common pool each member is allocated an equal share and is expected to contribute to the community according to his ability. Families have their own apartments, but there is a communal dining room and other facilities, and although each age-group of children is cared for as a unit, in most kibbutzim the children sleep in the family apartment. Variations in political colour are wide, and customs and living standards vary according to the background of the members and the financial and other progress made by the kibbutz, but generally speaking, the kibbutz movement has been proved to be, under certain conditions, an original and practical way of life.

The Jordan Valley, the southern edge of the Sea of Galilee and Kibbutz Degania, mother of the collective farms

Scenes from Kibbutz life ▶

"Go forth into the north country".   *Zechariah* 6:6.

LEAVING JERUSALEM towards the north, on the timeless Way of the Fathers, you quickly find yourself out of the traffic's hubbub and in quiet, rural surroundings. Before reaching the countryside, however, you pass through **Shuafat,** 'a district of handsome stone-built villas, while on a rise overlooking Shuafat's mansions is **Tel el-Ful,** the Gibeah of the Bible, "Gibeah which belongeth to Benjamin." (Judges 19:14). Saul, after being anointed by the prophet Samuel as Israel's first king, "went home to Gibeah," (I Samuel 10:26), and later built his palace there.

Excavations made in 1922 and again in 1933 by Professor W.F. Albright revealed a town of the time of the Judges, which had been razed by fire; above it was Saul's palace-citadel, and above that a ninth to eighth century BCE defence fort. What can be seen there at present, among fragmentary walls and trenches of the dig, are King Hussein of Jordan's preparations for the Summer Palace — preparations interrupted by the Six Day War.

West of Shuafat, observe the finger-like minaret of **Nebi Samuel** — the Prophet Samuel — where Samuel is said to be buried. Pointed arches and buttressed walls integrated into the mosque indicate Crusader origin, while inside the mosque, a cenotaph is set above Samuel's grave in the crypt below. Some authorities believe that here was biblical Ramah, where Samuel lived and died, and "all the Israelites.. lamented him and buried him in his house at Ramah." (I Samuel 25:1). Others place Ramah at er-Ram, a little to the east.

Close to Nebi Samuel is **el-Qubeibe,** the Emmaus of the New Testament, "a village... from Jerusalem about threescore furlongs." (Luke 24:13). Here the resurrected Jesus met Cleophas and Simon and, as the hour was late, Cleophas invited the stranger to his home, saying, "Abide with us; for it is toward evening and the day is far spent." (Luke 24:29). Inside the Franciscan church at Qubeibe is part of the House of Cleophas, while immediately outside is a complete Crusader village with streets, houses, and agricultural installations.

Neve Yaacov, a large post-Six Day War housing estate, recalls the little-known Jewish colony set up there in 1924 and named for Rabbi Yaacov Reiness. For 24 years, the members raised cattle and worked on afforestation — a Jewish island in an Arab sea — but in May 1948 they were forced to abandon their homes.

El-Jib, a picturesque Arab hamlet, stands on the Gibeon of 3500 years ago, where Joshua commanded the sun to "stand still upon Gibeon," (Joshua 10:12), so that he might finish off the battle in daylight. Joshua 10:2 describes it as "a great city, one of the royal cities," — the only Canaanite state to come to terms with the Israelites. At el-Jib is a unique rock-cut open pool of large dimensions — an unusual, spring-fed cistern where David's followers and those of Ish-boshet, Saul's son, "met together at the pool of Gibeon... and there was a very sore battle that day." (II Samuel 2:13-17). The Bible tells, too, how King Solomon "went to Gibeon to sacrifice there," (I Kings 3:4), and there he asked the Lord for "an understanding heart to judge thy people."

Professor J.B. Pritchard's dig of 1956 to 1959 unearthed this amazing pool, as well as a host of other interesting finds from this and other periods. Most significant were the wine cellars hewn into the rock, where 25,000 gallons (100,000 litres) of wine could be stored at one time. Earthenware jar handles stamped in archaic Hebrew script date this peak of prosperity to First Temple days.

Atarot, site of Jerusalem's airport, was formerly known as Kalandia. One

Ramallah

of the early attempts at hill farming was made here in 1914 by young Russian immigrants, including 19-year-old Levi Eshkol, Israel's premier from 1963 to 1969. Except for one brief interval, Jewish Atarot held out until 1948, when the whole village moved to the abandoned German colony of Wilhemina, near Lydda, now called Bnei Atarot.

Located on a hill-top nearly 1800 feet above sea level, pin-pointed by the soaring antennae of the relay station, Christian Arab **Ramallah** is a popular summer resort. Together with its Moslem twin-town of el-Bireh, famed for its natural fountains and rose gardens,

it has 26,000 inhabitants. El-Bireh is thought to be biblical Beeroth of the tribe of Benjamin, and although not mentioned by name, is traditionally where Mary and Joseph noticed the absence of the boy Jesus, and returned to look for him in the Temple.

As you journey on, note Beitin, the **Beth-el** of the Bible, where the Lord appeared to Jacob, who "called the name of that place Beth-el," (Genesis 28:19), or the House of God. Close by is Canaanite **Ai,** where excavations confirmed the statement in Joshua 8:28, that "Joshua burnt Ai, and made it... a desolation unto this day." On your left you pass the Crusader manor-house at **Jifna,** and further on, at the Arab village of **Sinjil,** or St. Gilles, was an important royal administrative borough of the Crusaders. On your right is Khirbet Seilun, biblical **Shiloh,** a time-honoured site of outstanding significance in the formation-time of Jewish history. A mile or two off the road, you find two mosques built on the foundations of an early third century CE synagogue, then the remains of two Byzantine churches. Little can be learnt on the spot from the trenches dug and walls exposed by the Danish expedition which worked here in 1926, but they found tra-

A flock of sheep grazing among the ancient olive groves with their shepherd

A new settlement in the hills of Samaria

ces of a settlement from the days of Abraham, and a thriving town from the period of the Judges. Joshua 18:1 tells how "the whole congregation of Israel assembled in Shiloh and set up the tabernacle," while I Samuel 1:3 describes how Elkanah and his barren wife, Hannah, "came to worship and sacrifice to the Lord of hosts in Shiloh." Their faith was rewarded by the birth of a son, Samuel, whom Hannah later brought "unto the house of the Lord in Shiloh."

For more than two centuries Shiloh was the hub of the infant nation, but when the Israelites "fetched the ark of the covenant out of Shiloh," (I Samuel 4:3), and lost it to the Philistines, Shiloh began to decline. It revived with the Return to Zion, and there was permanent habitation there during the Hasmonean, Herodian, Roman and Byzantine eras. Abandoned around 1300 CE, ancient Shiloh, the first home of the Tabernacle, where "the child Samuel grew before the Lord," (I Samuel 2-21), is a deserted waste.

Today, however, Jewish settlements like Shiloh, Ofra, Beth-el and many more, some founded by the Gush Emunim group, are reviving the olden days. Incidentally, Gush Emunim, which grew up after June 1967, comprises those who believe in establishing a Jewish Presence in all parts of biblical Israel. Mainly orthodox in outlook, there are others who share only the nationalistic angle.

Travelling through the Samarian hills, you cannot fail to observe remains of terraces, originally built up by the Israelites some 3000 years ago to increase the area of land available for planting. It was the Israelites, too, who invented a method of plastering water cisterns so that water could be stored throughout the year.

These artificial terraces were planted with olive trees and figs; with pomegranates and particularly with grapes, for vines flourish under these conditions of dryness and poor soil. Until today you can see acre upon acre of vines grown in this fashion, and although more modern appliances have replaced the rock-cut "gat," or winepress and the stone olive crusher, the principles of wine and of oil production remain the same.

Hill farming, successful as it is for indigenous fruits and for sheep rearing, cannot replace the wider spaces needed for the growing of grain. Valleys and plains were needed to supply the large quantities required, even in olden times. Nowadays, despite the many changes that have taken place in agriculture, and the proliferation of tractors and combines, you can often meet with simpler, more basic forms of husbandry.

You will sometimes come across a woman drawing water from a well as in biblical days; here and there

Scenes from Arab village life

Scenes from Arab village life

you may find a horse-drawn plough cutting a straight furrow; a wooden harrow with iron teeth scraping across a field, covering the recently-sown seed, or farmers winnowing grain by tossing it to the wind. These scenes are typical of the old-new Land of Israel, where modern technology and farming ways old as history exist, without conflict, side by side.

Continuing into the heart of Samaria, you see **Mount Gerizim** and **Mount Ebal** standing like sentinels on either side of Nablus and of its predecessor, Shechem. Barely 300 feet apart, Mount Gerizim to the south rises 2500 feet above sea level, while bleak Mount Ebal reaches nearly 3000 feet. These two mountains appear very early in Bible chronology, for as soon as Joshua entered the Promised Land, he "built an altar unto the Lord God of Israel in Mount Ebal... and wrote there upon the stones a copy of the law of Moses." (Joshua 8:30-33). Incidentally, the Samaritan version of the Torah, which the Samaritans claim is the correct one, changes Moses' injunction of Deuteronomy 27:4, to "set up these stones in Mount Ebal, and thou shalt plaster them with plaster," by replacing Mount Ebal by Mount Gerizim.

The **Samaritans,** who at the dawn of the Christian era were counted in their hundreds of thousands, today number scarcely 500 souls, half of whom live in Nablus, at the foot of Mount Gerizim, and half in Holon, near Tel Aviv. Claiming direct descent from Ephraim and Manasseh, Joseph's sons, they rather resent the name by which they are known, and prefer to be called Shamerim, or Guardians, for they contend they have guarded the Law of Moses, keeping it pure and unsullied down the generations. They further claim that, when Israel fell to the Assyrians in 721 BCE, only a fraction of the indigenous population was captured, the rest stayed on, and were the ancestors of the present Samaritans.

Only the Pentateuch is accepted as the Holy Writ, and all its precepts are

The Samaritan High Priest with
the Scroll of the Torah

Nablus (Shechem), lying between Mount Gerizim and Mount Ebal

meticulously honoured. Mount Gerizim, not Mount Moriah, is considered the Holy Mountain, where Adam and Eve were created from the dust of the ground, and where Isaac was bound for sacrifice. On the whole, the Samaritan bible adheres closely to the accepted text, the most controversial difference being the telescoping of the first two commandments into one, and the replacement of the tenth commandment by one stressing the sanctity of Mount Gerizim.

Mount Gerizim is the focus of the three pilgrim festivals of the Samaritans. Their Passover festival, re-enacting the biblical scenes of the slaughter and roasting of the pascal lambs, with each man obeying the order that, "ye shall eat it in haste, with your loins girded, your shoes on your feet, and your staff in your hand" (Exodus 12:11), is particularly memorable.

The Samaritan Temple erected on Mount Gerizim rivalled the Temple of Jerusalem until it was destroyed by Hasmonean ruler, John Hyrcanus, in 128 BCE. Roman emperor Hadrian built a pagan temple to Jupiter above its ruins, and over that two Byzantine churches arose. An interesting investigation made by Dr. Robert Bull of the American School of Oriental Research in 1968 revealed relics of the original temple of the Samaritans.

On the border of Mount Gerizim, in the village of Askar, biblical Sychar, is the **Well of Jacob,** dug by the Patriarch over 3000 years ago. John 4:5-6 tells the story of how Jesus came "to a city of Samaria, which is called Sychar... now Jacob's well was there," and here, "being wearied with his journey, sat thus on the well," and met the woman of Samaria. Considered a hallowed spot from early in the fourth century, when a church was put up over the well, it has remained a place of pilgrimage ever since.

At nearby Balata are the gigantic ruins of ancient **Shechem.** Work carried out at intervals from 1913 to 1964 revealed a settlement of 6000 years ago, and evidence that during the Patriarchal age and after, Shechem was a great and important city. "Abram passed through the land unto the place of Sichem," you read in Genesis 12:6, and further on, in Genesis 33:18, that "Jacob came to Shalem, a city of Shechem, in the land of Canaan." Relations between Jacob's family and the

"That thou shalt put the blessing upon Mount Gerizim and the curse upon Mount Ebal"
(Deut. 11, 29)

Jacob's Well, Nablus

was moved to well-watered **Tirza,** where Omri reigned six years before buying "the hill Samaria of Shemer for two talents of silver, and he built on the hill, and called the name of the city... Samaria," (I Kings 16:24), transferring his seat there in 880 BCE.

When the kings of Israel moved their palace to Samaria, Shechem gradually declined until, with the Hasmonean conquest, it was abandoned. Rebuilt two hundred years later as Roman Neapolis, or **Nablus,** a Samaritan centre and a colony for demobilized Roman soldiers, it developed with the development of Christianity. Under the early Arabs and the Crusaders, Nablus thrived, and today it is the main town of the district of Samaria, with a population of about 45,000, mostly Moslem Arabs.

The royal city of **Samaria,** of which rich remains were found, was overrun by the Assyrians in 721 BCE; it was then rebuilt by Alexander of Macedon as a Greek town, and again rebuilt by Herod, who changed its name to Sebaste. Here he married the Hasmonean princess, beautiful Mariamne, and here he murdered her and their two sons, Alexander and Aristobolus. Under Roman rule, it continued to be a magnificent city, but as Nablus pros-

native Hivites were strained by the tale of rapine, murder and broken promises related in Genesis 34. Joshua "gathered all the tribes of Israel to Shechem," (Joshua 24:1), and "made a covenant with the people that day, and set them a statute and an ordinance in Shechem," (Joshua 24:25).

During the government of the Judges, Shechem continued to be a town of consequence, and the background of a political struggle for power after Gideon's death. One of Gideon's sons by a concubine from Shechem was Abimelech, who conspired with his mother's kin to kill his 70 brothers, and they "made Abimelech king in the plains of the pillar that was in Shechem." (Judges 9:6). Only the youngest son, Jotham, escaped.

Under David and Solomon, Shechem was part of the United Monarchy. On Solomon's death, however, Israel split off, with Jeroboam as its king and Shechem as its capital. Soon the capital

Ancient Shechem

The Roman Theatre at Sebastia

A columned street, Sebastia

pered, Samaria fell into obscurity. What you see now are the impressive partly-restored Greek, Herodian and Roman relics excavated by the expeditions of 1908 to 1910, and of 1931 to 1935.

Travelling north from Nablus, you pass biblical **Dothan,** where "Joseph went after his brothers and found them in Dothan," (Genesis 37:17), and "they stripped him of his coat of many colours and cast him into the pit." Continue on the way to Megiddo, looking out meanwhile for **Jenin,** the Engannem of the Bible, now an Arab town of 14,000, and **Taanach,** a Cana-

Roman ruins at Sebastia

anite city-state conquered by Joshua. **Megiddo,** mentioned in the Egyptian writings of the fifteenth century BCE, was also one of the walled city-states taken by Joshua. Rich and powerful under the United Monarchy, I Kings 9:15 recalls how Solomon raised a levy to build "the wall of Jerusalem, and Hazor, and Megiddo, and Gezer." Ahaziah, king of Judah, "fled to Megiddo and died there," (II Kings 9:27), and Josiah, too, fell in battle there in 610 BCE, and "his servants carried him in a chariot dead from Megiddo." (II Kings 23:30).

Upon this strategic hill-top, expertly excavated in 1925 by the Oriental Institute of the University of Chicago, you will find a partially restored walled town with fine gates, as well as remarkable explanatory models. On the site itself you see the stepped water shaft leading to the water source; the Canaanite temple; the stables, palaces and storehouses, the sentry towers and soldiers' quarters. Many of

The water system at Megiddo

Megiddo (Armageddon) viewed from the sunflower fields of the Jezreel Valley

The Jezreel Valley viewed from
the Balfour Forest

guarding the mountain pass and often in conflict with invading armies, it is not surprising that Christian folklore holds that Megiddo, or Armageddon, will be the final battleground of all time in the struggle between good and evil.

A short way off is **Afula,** the urban and commercial centre of the Valley of Jezreel, once the Crusader castle of La Feve, of which practically nothing is left. A busy road junction and market town, it has never lived up to the promise it showed when established in 1925. However, from Afula you can quickly reach Nazareth, Mount Tabor, and Tsippori.

Nazareth in Galilee, where Jesus spent his childhood, is now a town with a population of 42,000, mostly Christian Arabs, while on the height above is Upper Nazareth, an immigrant township founded in 1957 and housing some 23,000 Jews. Old Nazareth's winding, cobbled lanes; its churches, convents and monasteries, and

the objects found are exhibited in the small museum. With Megiddo's history of battles and bloodshed, always

Partial view of Nazareth, with the Church of the Annunciation in the centre

The Church of the Annunciation

Nazareth market scene

The "Davrat" road-side restaurant

The Church of the Transfiguration on Mount Tabor

the all-pervading sense of history vividly conjure up the story of 2000 years ago, in which Joseph, heeding the angel's words, "took the young child and his mother... and came and dwelt in a city called Nazareth" (Matthew 2:21-23). It seems to have been an ordinary place, with a Jewish community that was almost wiped out by the Romans during the Jewish revolt, but was revived in Talmudic times. A Crusader district centre, it was again overrun by the Saracens, then rebuilt much as it is to-day, beginning in the seventeenth century of this era.

Nazareth has a wealth of holy sites. There is Mary's Well, close to the Church of St. Gabriel, the Greek Orthodox Church of the Annunciation; the grand new Basilica of the Annunciation, owned by the Franciscans and covering most interesting remains of earlier churches; the Church of Joseph, built above his home and workshop; the Synagogue-Church where Jesus, "as his custom was, went... on the sabbath day," (Luke 4:16); and the Chapel of Our Lady's Fear, from whence Mary is said to have watched

Mount Tabor

Interior of the Church of the Transfiguration

Jesus being "led unto the brow of the hill, to be cast down," (Luke 4:29). On the summit of **Mount Tabor,** the Mount of the Transfiguration, stands Antonio Barluzzi's Basilica of the Transfiguration, skilfully incorporating earlier church relics. This is the same Mount Tabor from where, at the prophetess Deborah's behest, "Barak went down from mount Tabor, and ten thousand men after him," (Judges 4: 14), to fight Jabin king of Hatzor. Josephus Flavius, who for a time commanded the Jewish forces in Galilee against the Romans, writes of his citadel on Tabor, and his strong fortress walls encircling the hill can still be traced.

Nearby is **Nain,** where Jesus restored a widow's dead son to life (Luke 7:11), and **Kfar Kana,** scene of the miracle at Cana, when Jesus said, "Fill the water pots with water," (John 2:7), and the water became wine. Here are two churches, one Greek Orthodox and one Franciscan, where among some interesting archaeological finds can be

General view of Nain

A Turkish fort made of Roman sarcophagi crowns the hill, while around it a Roman amphitheatre and other structures have been unearthed. Rabbi Yehuda Ha'Nasi, compiler of the Mishnah, lived and died here, and his grave is here, although another attributed to him is in Beit Shearim. A synagogue floor with an Aramaic blessing is in the Crusader church.

Returning to Tiberias, note the double-peaked **Horns of Hattin,** where the Crusaders met a decisive defeat at the hands of Saladin in 1187. On the opposite hill, at sea level but rising 600 feet above the Sea of Galilee, is orthodox **Kibbutz Lavi,** established in 1949 by 50 members of a British youth movement. Undeterred by the bleak,

seen a mosaic inscription in Aramaic from a Talmudic synagogue on the site.

Tsippori, or Sepphoris, was for the Christian era, the largest city in Galilee, traditionally the home of Mary's parents, Anne and Joachim, and the birthplace of Mary. Tsippori's citizens did not resist the Romans, thus escaping the fate which befell so many towns. Renamed by the Romans Diocaesarea, it soon became a famed centre of learning, and was the seat of the Sanhedrin from 170 to 200 CE.

Kfar Kana, the water jar

General view of Kfar Kana

stony land allotted to them, they cleared the stones, dug for water, planted and built. Now its 400 joint owners farm 2500 acres, run an excellent Guest House, and have a successful carpentry shop. Their synagogue, inspired by the early Galilean synagogues, is a gem.

Kibbutz Lavi Guest House

The Horns of Hittin

A reservoir of the national water carrier

Afula, capital of the Jezreel Valley

Around the Sea of Galilee

"From the plain to the Sea of Chinneroth".   *Joshua 12:3.*

THE SEA OF GALILEE, where Jesus preached and Talmudic sages taught and studied, lies 600 feet below sea level. Called **Lake Kinneret**, biblical Chinneroth, from the Hebrew word, "kinnor," a harp or lyre, referring to its unusual shape, it measures 14 miles in length, is about 8 miles across, and its average depth is 150 feet. Fed by the River Jordan flowing in from the north, as well as by sweetwater underground springs, the lake acts as a reservoir for the National Water Carrier.

On the south-western edge of Lake Kinneret is **Tiberias,** capital of Lower Galilee, founded around 20 CE by Herod Antipas, son of Herod the Great, on the site of ancient Rakkath, mentioned in Joshua 19:35 as a fenced city, together with Hammath and Kinneret. Planned in the Greek style, independent and allowed to formulate its own laws and mint its own coins, in 67 CE it peaceably surrendered to the Romans. With the fall of Jerusalem three years later, Jews flocked to Tiberias. Schools of religious learning were set up, much work was done on the Mishnah and the Jerusalem Talmud, and Tiberias became one of the four holy cities of Palestine. For a time the Sanhedrin convened here, and soon the population numbered an astounding 40,000!

Although within the sphere of Jesus' ministry, Christianity made little headway in Tiberias until the sixth century, under the late Byzantines. Conquered by the Arabs in 636 CE, then by the Crusaders who remained in power from 1100 to 1247, and utilized by both as an administrative centre, the town nevertheless steadily declined right through the Middle Ages. In 1562, Portuguese Don Joseph and his mother-in-law, Donna Grazia, unsuccessfully attempted to revive Jewish Tiberias. Only in the eighteenth century under the Bedouin chief Daher el-Amar, did the city begin to grow again. The 1948 War of Independence left 4000 Jews in an all-Jewish Tiberias, which today is prosperous and thriving, with a population of nearly 30,000 Jews.

Weathered walls of black basalt give Tiberias its typical appearance. Those you see at present, although restored by Daher el-Amar in 1738, are basically Crusader, and can be traced north from the tower adjoining the Greek Orthodox monastery on the lake shore to the citadel now called the Donna Grazia complex of restaurants and galleries. The area of the Crusader town was about 37 acres, far smaller than the 200 acres covered by Herodian Tiberias, which stretched southward from the present

General view of Tiberias from the east, with the tomb of Rabbi Meir Baal Haness in the foreground

Tiberias, the promenade

Tiberias, Hot Springs

Greek Orthodox monastery to Hammath.

An ideal winter resort, its temperature never drops below 14 degrees centigrade, and the number of rainy days annually is less than 50. In and around Tiberias are a number of excellent hotels, as well as many beautiful

Tiberias

bathing and recreation beaches, and it is warm enough for water sports — swimming, water-skiing, and speedboat racing to be indulged in all the year round. Sight-seeing in the town may include the Museum of Antiquities, housed in an abandoned mosque; the Church of St. Peter, shaped like a boat; the Tomb of Rabbi Moses Maimonides — the Rambam — who was buried here in 1204, and the hillslope grave of Rabbi Akiba, who met a martyr's death at the hands of the Romans in 135 CE.

South of Tiberias is **Hammath Tiberias**, its hot mineral springs making it into a health-giving spa, as popular today as it was with the Roman officials and their families nearly 2000 years back. A dig made adjoining the springs in 1961 revealed Roman buildings and the remains of four synagogues. At the lowest level was a synagogue of the third century CE, and above it one from the fourth century, with an exquisite mosaic floor still in place. Near the south-pointing apse is a panel showing Jewish ritual objects; the middle panel pictures a Zodiac wheel, with one of the four seasons represented at each corner, and near the entrance are Greek and Aramaic inscriptions blessing those who donated to the synagogue. Remains of two larger prayer halls — one from the sixth-seventh century and one from the seventh-eighth century — were discovered in the same spot. Above, the hot springs is the Tomb of Rabbi Meir Baal Ha'Ness, a second century rabbi nicknamed the Miracle Worker.

Travelling north from Tiberias along the western shore of the lake, you see on your left the towering cliffs of Mount Arbel, referred to in Hosea 10: 14 as the "battlefield of Beit-arbel."

Here in 39 BCE, Herod launched an all-out campaign against the Zealots who had entrenched themselves in the caves, and Josephus tells a tragic story of a father who killed his seven children, his wife and himself rather than be taken captive. At the outlet of the Arbel Valley is **Migdal-Nuniyeh,** or Magdala, home of Mary Magdalen, from whom Jesus "cast seven devils," (Luke 8:2), and who became one of his most devoted followers. Close to Migdal is the secluded Peniel-by-Galilee beach and hostel of the Jerusalem Young Men's Christian Association.

Tiberias, mosaic floor of the ancient Hamat synagogue   **Water sports**

The old city wall of Tiberias

Mount Arbel

"Nof Ginossar" Guest House

Lakeside **Kibbutz Ginossar,** green and fertile, was established in 1937, and is now a veritable paradise, with lawns bordered by shrubs and flowers, and quiet inlets where ducks nest and swans glide along the streams. Nof Ginossar Guest House has all the comforts of a good hotel, and is an excellent starting point for the many excursions available in the vicinity. Very near is **Wadi Amud,** where the skull of the Galilean Man of 100,000 years ago was found in a cave, while on the water's edge is **Khirbet Min-yeh,** the ruins of a Winter Palace of an eighth century caliph.

Jesus' ministry comes to life at **Tab-gha** — in Greek, Heptapecon or Seven Springs — the traditional site of the Miracle of the Loaves and Fishes. Gospel stories tell how 5000 people gathered to hear Jesus' words, and stayed until nightfall. "Give ye them to eat," said Jesus to his apostles. They answered, "We have no more but five loaves and two fishes," (Luke 9.13). Jesus blessed the food, and it sufficed for all.

The table-rock where this wonder took place has been the altar of successive churches, the earliest, built in the fourth century CE, being overbuilt

Tabgha, Church of St. Peter's Primacy, Mensa Domini

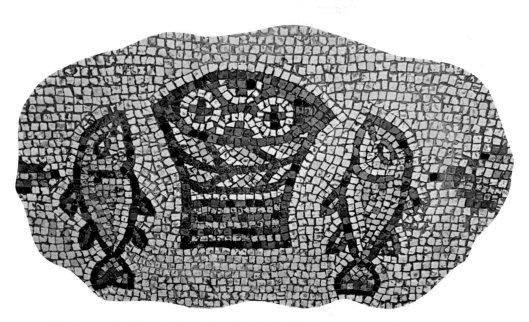

Tabgha, mosaic floor in the Church of the Multiplication of the Loaves and Fishes

a century later by a larger structure, the mosaic pavement of which is still there. A modern miracle, at Tel Kinneret, near Tabgha, is the underground station of the **National Water Carrier,** which starts the waters of the Sea of Galilee on their 85-mile uphill journey to Rosh Ha'Ayin the headsprings of the Yarkon River.

Further along the shore is the **Sanctuary of the Primacy,** or Mensa Christi — the Table of Christ. This simple chapel marks where Jesus, after the resurrection, "showed himself again to his disciples at the sea of Tiberias," (John 21:1), and they ate together. He then appointed Simon Peter to the office of the Primacy, with the words, "Feed my sheep." (John 21:16). Built by the Franciscans on Byzantine foundations, the church is located on a small quay with rock-hewn steps on which Jesus is said to have stood as he looked over the water.

Between Tabgha and Capernaum, on a slight rise, is the **Mount of the Beatitudes,** where Jesus is said to have preached the Sermon on the Mount. Remains of a small Byzantine church

were disclosed here in 1935, but the Franciscans chose to rebuild the modern Church of the Beatitudes on the hill-top, not actually on the ancient chapel. Constructed in 1938, again by Antonio Barluzzi, the octagonal church, recalling the eight blessings, is also a pilgrim hostel — a quiet haven overlooking the placid blue waters of the lake.

St. Peter's Fish

Capernaum's white limestone synagogue is a symbol to both Jews and Christians. A wealthy Jewish town in Roman days, as evidenced by this majestic structure, Matthew 4:12 tells how Jesus "departed into Galilee, and leaving Nazareth, came and dwelt in Capernaum." Perhaps the most elaborate of the early Galilean synagogues, its soaring columns, ashlars decorated with floral and other motifs including one of the mobile ark, and its inscribed pillars are remarkably interesting.

When acquired by the Franciscans in 1891, this was nothing but wasteland strewn with engraved stones being burnt into quicklime by the Bedouin.

A fence was immediately put up, and by 1926 the synagogue was partially restored, and the traditional St. Peter's House-Synagogue had been discovered beneath the Byzantine Octagonal Church west of the main building.

A little inland is the black basalt second century CE synagogue of **Korazin.** Here, the story goes, the Jews of the town refused to allow Jesus to

Aerial view of the Mount of Beatitudes, showing the northern shores of the Sea of Galilee

Ruins of the ancient synagogue at Capernaum

Capernaum, aerial view of the excavated area. From right to left: the synagogue, ruins of first century houses and the fifth century church built over the traditional house of St. Peter

Reconstruction of the Synagogue

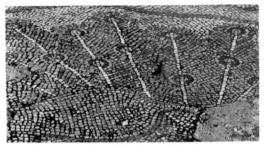

Part of an ancient mosaic floor

Relief of the Star of David

Relief of a Palm Tree

An ancient mill-stone

The Jordan Park

Ruins of the ancient synagogue at Korazin

preach, and Luke 10:13-15 recalls the curse laid upon the unrepentant cities, with the words, "Woe unto thee, Chorazin! woe unto thee Beitsaida... and thou Capernaum, shalt be thrust down to hell." First excavated in 1905, when the three great portals and a wealth of carved friezes, cornices and capitals were unearthed, later digs were made in 1926 and 1968, when houses, streets and ritual baths attached to the synagogue were found. Korazin seems to have been destroyed by an earthquake in

The River Jordan flowing into the Sea of Galilee through the Beticha Valley

Kursi (Gergesa), remains of the ancient Byzantine Church

The Ostrich farm at Kibbutz Ha'On

Aerial view of Kibbutz Ein Gev on the shores of the Sea of Galilee

the third century, and was never rebuilt.

North from Korazin is **Almagor,** founded in 1961 as a border defence post and now a moshav based on mixed farming. A memorial nearby commemorates the seven members of Almagor who were ambushed and killed by the Syrians in the early 1960's. Beyond, at the entrance of the River Jordan into the lake, is the **Beticha Valley,** a lush, jungle-like area interlaced with rivulets bringing in an abundance of water. Close to it is biblical **Beitsaida,** the village and **Beit Ha'Bek** where, amid groves of eucalyptus trees, a group of Russian Jews tried to establish a fishing village as early as 1905. A short way inland, easily reached from the north-eastern corner of the lake, is **Breichat Ha'Meshushim,** a strange, deep pool of clear bubbling water made up of six-sided crystalline rock formations.

On the east bank of the Sea of Galilee is **Ein Gev,** a kibbutz founded here in 1937, when conditions were incredibly hard and the only approach was by boat from Tiberias. Fishing was then, as it is now, the main occupation, making the years between 1948 and 1967 particularly difficult, for Syrian soldiers stationed immediately to the north and east, threatened the daily life and livelihood of the members. Today Ein Gev is prosperous and safe. Plantations of dates and bananas bring in a good income, as does the fish restaurant, which is a "must" for every tourist, but Ein Gev is best known for its annual Passover Music Festival, which is a great attraction.

On a hill above the Kibbutz stands **Susita** — the Greek Hippos — a rich and powerful, well-fortified city conquered by Hasmonean king Alexander Yannai in the first century BCE. Later given to Herod by his Roman overlords, it continued to be a thriving non-Jewish city throughout Roman and Byzantine times. Rows of huge granite pillars, Greek votary inscriptions, and massive church foundations can still be seen, as well as traces of the town walls, houses and paved streets, and numerous cisterns.

A little north of Susita, on the lake shore, are the ruins of **Kursi,** the New Testament Gergesa, or Gadara, where Jesus met two men possessed of devils. He miraculously cast the devils out of the men into a herd of swine which stampeded into the water and was drowned.

For centuries, the site of Kursi was a mystery, but it was accidentally discovered soon after the Six Day War, when a bulldozer clearing the way for a new road found a Byzantine basilica measuring 72 by 135 feet, with a fine mosaic floor. Attached to it was a chapel and a fortified monastery of the fifth, sixth and seventh centuries, while in a well-preserved barrel-roofed crypt were the skeletons of more than 30 middle-aged males, additional proof that this was a monastery.

A recent addition to the pilgrim sites of the Sea of Galilee is the Place of Baptism near Degania A, where the Jordan leaves the lake. Tradition claims that here Jesus "was baptized of John in Jordan." Mark 1:9

Windsurfing on the Sea of Galilee

The Galilee Boat
This ancient boat was discovered at low tide of the Sea of Galilee during the drought year of 1985, and is believed to be a fisherman's boat dating back to 70–20 B.C.

"Yardenit", Pilgrims' Site of Baptism

Upper Galilee and the Golan.

"It is a land of hills and valleys, and drinketh water of the rain of heaven."

Deuteronomy 11:11.

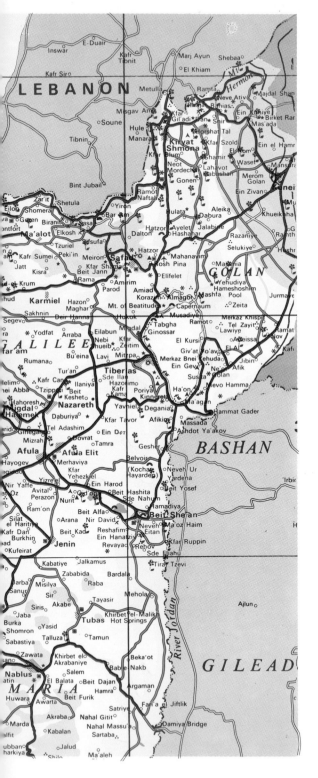

HIGH ON A MOUNTAIN TOP, more than 3000 feet above sea level, is **Safed,** capital of Upper Galilee. One of Israel's four sacred cities, Safed is also known as the City of Mysticism, the home of the Cabbala — a mediaeval philosophy of direct communication between Man and the Almighty — whose founder and chief exponent was sixteenth century Rabbi Isaac Luria, also called Ha'Ari, or the Lion. Today an all-Jewish town of some 15,000 people, it is a favourite summer resort, while Safed's clean air and combination of wonderful panoramas with narrow, stepped streets and vine-covered courtyards has attracted a colony of sculptors and artists.

Safed, partial view with the artists' colony and Mount Meron

A lane in the old city of Safed

The "Ari" Synagogue

General view of Meron

Few references to Safed are found until the end of the Second Temple period when, due to its strategic position, it was fortified by Josephus Flavius as one of the key fortresses of the north. Its ruins, upon which the Crusader castle of Saphet was later built, can be seen on Citadel Hill, now a municipal park.

Within a hundred years of the ousting of the Crusaders, Safed saw an intellectual revival. Its Jews gained reinforcements from the refugees who fled from the Spanish Inquisition, and the Middle Ages brought in a religious and spiritual flowering of the hill-top city. Here lived outstanding figures in Jewish life and literature — Rabbi Joseph Caro, who wrote the "Shulchan Aruch," — the Set Table,– around 1555; Rabbi Haim Vitale; Rabbi Moses Cordovero, and Rabbi Jacob Biraw, who planned to restore the Sanhedrin. Here the first Hebrew printing press in the Middle East was initiated in 1563 — a tremendous step forward in the dissemination of learn-

The Guest House at Kibbutz Ayelet Ha'Shahar

Ruins of the ancient synagogue at Baram

The ancient watersystem at Hazor

ing and language. You can spend an interesting day or two in Safed visiting the Printing Museum, the Glicenstein Art Museum, the Artists' Quarter, Citadel Hill, and the profusion of synagogues and hallowed tombs.

Meron, a small Jewish village set up in 1949, stands on the site of a Talmudic era settlement with the impressive remains of a Second Century CE synagogue. Near Meron are the graves of famous rabbis, notably Rabbi Shimon ben Yohai and his son, Eliezer; Rabbi Hillel, and Rabbi Yohanan Ha'Sandlar. Each Lag b'Omer — between the festivals of Passover and the Feast of Weeks — a mass pilgrimage is made from Safed to the tomb of Rabbi Shimon, a noted Cabbalist. Bonfires are lit, and prayers offered up all through the night.

The first of the Jewish settlements of Galilee, **Rosh Pina** — the Headstone, or Cornerstone — was founded in 1879. Pleasantly rural, with cobbled streets and individual houses with gardens, it is still little more than a hamlet, with about 1000 people living there. It has, however, been given new importance by the airfield recently opened at neighbouring Mahanaim. **Ayelet Ha'Shahar,** a well-established kibbutz of 60 years standing, is noted for its Guest House and for its unique museum of finds from adjoining **Tel Hazor.** Hazor was perhaps the largest of the Canaanite city-states, and strongly resisted the incursions of the children of Israel. Joshua 11:10 relates how he "took Hazor, and smote the King thereof with the sword; for Hazor was the head of all those kingdoms". Joshua also "burnt Hazor with fire," (Joshua 11:11).

Archaeological excavations were carried out on the mound by J. Garstang, of Liverpool University, in 1928, then on a wider scale by Professor Yigael Yadin in 1955. Occupation from the third millenium BCE was brought to light, but the earliest large settlement dated from the eighteenth-seventeenth centuries BCE. Above this were four

The Trumpeldor Memorial

The Huleh Wild Life Reserve

Canaanite strata of good-sized towns, sometimes spread over 200 acres, the last of which was destroyed by Joshua around 1250 BCE.

Later came the Solomonic city, with massive walls and gates, razed by the Assyrians, after which only small settlements were found on the tel, the last being from the second century BCE. A recent discovery was the Solomonic water supply system, with a broad shaft and stepped tunnel leading down to the water source.

Canaanite Hazor's golden age was from about 1550 to 1250 BCE. Finds from this period and from the layer below included a regal palace and a number of temples with remarkable stelae and cult objects. Here was found the basalt lion, symbol of Hazor. Incidentally, one of Hazor's chief functions of that time was as a communication centre. From here caravan routes fanned out in all directions, one of the most important being over the **Bridge of Jacob's Daughters** — a ford in olden days — which did, and does still, cross the Jordan on the way to Syria.

Journeying northward, you reach the 600 acre **Huleh Nature Reserve,** the last remnant of the Huleh swamps, once teeming with water buffalo and wild boar, turtles and other water creatures, rare fish and wading birds living a primeval existence among the aquatic plants and creepers. The Reserve recalls how the 12,000 acres of

The Good Fence, Metulla

the Huleh area looked before it was drained by the Jewish National Fund in the 1950's and transformed into fertile fields.

Further north is the immigrant town of **Kiryat Shmoneh,** named for the national hero, Joseph Trumpeldor, and his seven companions. Market-place and shopping centre for the district, it has a population of rather less than 20,000. Close by is **Kfar Giladi,** a Kibbutz founded in 1916, with a comfortable Guest House, while near it is a memorial to Trumpeldor and his comrades who, in 1920, fell at the hands of Arabs attacking the settlement of Tel Hai.

Passing through the **Ayun Nature Reserve,** with the Tannur waterfall, streams and shady groves, you reach the 80-year-old townlet of **Metulla ,** on the Lebanese border. Metulla , with its cottages and colourful gardens, its leisurely atmosphere and old-world charm, is a summer refuge for city-dwellers.

General view of Kiryat Shmoneh

The River Jordan and snow-covered Mount Hermon

Castle Nimrod (Kalaat Namrud), a Crusader fortress on the slopes of Mount Hermon

Another Nature Reserve, **Horshat Tal,** dotted with ancient oaks amidst a network of ice-cold brooks fed by the snows of Mount Hermon, is near biblical **Tel Dan.** Professor Avram Biran directs an on-going dig there since 1965, and among many other discoveries, has exposed a gigantic Bronze Age glacis and a unique 2000 BCE city gate. Here, too, an open-air temple was found, maybe "a house of high places," (I Kings 12:31), where the Golden Calf might possibly have been worshipped by back-sliding King Jeroboam of Israel, for 1 Kings 12:28-29 tells how Jeroboam "made two calves of gold... and set the one in Beth-el, and the other put he in Dan."

The **Golan Heights,** or Ramat Ha'Golan, from which, before 1967, Syrian troops would threaten the peaceful Jewish fields and orchards of the Jordan Valley and the eastern bank of Lake Kinneret, are now under Israeli rule. These black basalt, volcanic mountains, which extend from 9200 feet high Mount Hermon in a broad arc east and south to the Yarmuk Valley, were allotted to the half tribe of Manasseh, to whom, according to Joshua 21:27, "they gave Golan in Bashan."

Before visiting the beauty spots and historical sites of the Golan Heights, look over the Syrian bunkers and well-entrenched gun emplacements ready to attack Israel, which were he-roically stormed and seized by the Israel Defence Army in June 1967.

The spring of **Banias,** one of the sources of the River Jordan, issues from a deep cave. Hillocks, rivulets and luscious growth create a beautiful setting for the pagan temple of Pan, with

The Banias spring, one of the three sources of the Jordan

Ramot Holiday Village

Birket Ram

its Greek-inscribed votary niches. Here are the ruins of Caesarea Philippi, built by Philip, Herod's son by one of his Jewish wives, Cleopatra, and of the Crusader castle Belinas, while on the height above is **Castle Nimrod,** or Kalat el-Subeiba, a well-preserved fortress with round towers and huge underground cisterns. Kalat el-Subeiba was built as a hideout for a peculiar Moslem sect, the Assassins, or Hashashim, part of whose life-style was the taking of hashish. In 1129 the castle was given over to King Baldwin II of Jerusalem in return for his protection.

From Castle Nimrod, a path leads up to Ramot Shalom where, weather permitting, you can ski on the slopes of Mount Hermon. You can also see **Birket Ram,** a round, very deep fresh water pool located some 3000 feet above sea level. Birket Ram, measuring about 3000 feet across, is something of a mystery, for it has no visible inlet or outlet. **Kuneitra,** not far off, was a road junction and district command centre, but it is no longer under Israeli jurisdiction.

Ramat Ha'Golan is filled with new set-

The Huleh Valley and the Golan Heights, with snow-covered Mount Hermon on the left

El Hama, Alligator Park

El Hama, the mineral water falls

tlements — mainly of religious youth — and numerous remains of early synagogues and Batei Midrash, or Houses of Study, witnessing an active Jewish presence in the Golan during the first centuries of the Christian era. Among the new groups are Meron Golan, the first kibbutz to go out near Kuneitra in 1970, Afik, El-iad, Geshur, Bnei Yehuda, Ramot Magshimim, Mevo Hamma and others. Mevo Hamma is near historical **Hammat Gader,** its hot springs known from Second Temple days. Hammat Gader has now been transformed into an unusual recreation spot. Bathing pools filled with hot spring water — 52 degrees centigrade, (or 125 fahrenheit)are set among green gardens, picnic tables and barbecue grills.

Adjacent is a fifth century synagogue floor, with many inscriptions in Aramaic and Greek,while renewed work on the Roman baths nearer the Yarmuk has produced amazing results, unearthing perhaps the largest complex of bathhouses in the whole of the Roman empire. A rare find is a mosaic pavement with a poem by the

Hammat Gader (El Hama) and the Yarmuk River

Ruins of the Synagogue at Gamla

Byzantine empress Eudocia, who lived in Jerusalem in the fifth century. To add fun and colour, alligators brought in from Florida bask happily in shallow, enclosed ponds.

Synagogue remains have also been found at Fik, Ein Sem-sem, Ein Zivan, Dabura, Kfar Haruv and other places, but perhaps most moving is that at **Gamla,** where a perfect first century

CE synagogue has been uncovered at the Zealot fortress of Gamla — the Masada of the north — excavated by

Skiing on Mount Hermon

Kazrin, the new town on the Golan Heights

Kibbutz Gonen

Kibbutz Kfar Giladi Guest House

Kibbutz Hagoshrim Guest House

Shmariyahu Guttman. When the Romans were approaching in 68 CE, thousands of Gamla's defenders killed themselves and their families rather than be captured.

In the Upper Galilee, with its beautiful scenery and pleasant weather, there are many kibbutz Guest Houses, which almost every tourist visits.

Picnicking by the roadside in the Upper Galilee

Kibbutz Kfar Blum Guest House

Westward from Jerusalem

"Even unto the Great Sea westward."
Joshua 23 : 4

The Latrun Monastery

LEAVING JERUSALEM TOWARDS the west, you find yourself travelling along the **Valley of Ayalon** where Joshua, coming to the aid of Canaanite Gibeon, bade the sun "Stand still upon Gibeon, and thou, Moon, in the valley of Ayalon." (Joshua 10:12). This strategic pass is the capital's lifeline — to Lod, the skyway to Europe, America and other parts of the globe — and the shortest route to the Mediterranean, the Great Sea.

For 19 years, from 1948 to 1967, this was the only road to and from Jerusalem, for those to the north, east and south were blocked by the Jordanians. Of the utmost importance to the safety of Jerusalem, this valley has been the scene of frequent warfare. Here were fought many of the battles between the Greeks and the Maccabees, while relics of Roman fortresses dotted along the way witness how essentially important it was then. The early Arabs, the Crusaders, the Turks and the British brought in their military might through the same road, while much blood was shed in the War of Liberation to keep this fateful passage open. You first notice **Mei Neftoah,** or Lifta, with a large natural spring and in-

Kibbutz Maale Hahamisha, in the Judean Hills

teresting Crusader ruins, then **Motza,** where remains of a Roman guard tower can be seen as you drive past. A side turning brings you to **Beit Zayit,** a thriving smallholders' and residential village, where the extremely rare phenomenon of fossilized Dinosaur footprints of a hundred million years back can be seen by the central silo.

Mount Castel, also with ruins of a Roman citadel, saw desperate fighting during the 1948 war, fortunately resulting in an Israeli victory. Another track on the left leads to Ein Hemed, or **Aqua Bella,** where a recreation area has been set up in the spring-fed, park-like grounds of a fortified Crusader convent. On the right are twin kibbutzim — **Kiryat Anavim and Maale Ha'Hamisha** — each with its own swimming pool and Guest House.

Abu Ghosh, the biblical "Kirjath-jearim, a city of the children of Judah," (Joshua 18:14), had its place in the wanderings of the Ark, for after it was sent away by the Philistines, "the ark abode in Kirjath-jearim... for twenty years." (I Samuel 7:2). Now by-passed by the new freeway, Abu Ghosh is an Arab hamlet of some 2000 people, which has always been friendly towards Israel. There are two interesting sites in the village — the Convent of the Ark of the Covenant, built on the hill summit over a very early mosaic floor, and the Crusader church in the valley, erected on Roman foundations.

At **Shaar Ha'Gai,** the Gate of the Valley or Bab el-Wad where the Judean uplands meet the plain, look out for the Turkish khan and the small Turkish guard tower behind the service station. Look out, too, for the symbolic wrecks of armoured cars and lorries burned by the Arab Legion as they attempted to break the siege of beleaguered Jerusalem.

Since 1967, the road runs straight through to the coast, but during the 1948 to 1967 interval, when the stretch between Latrun and Ramle was in enemy hands, a by-pass was quickly cut through the Judean foothills. This less

Shaar Hagai (Bab el-Wad), burnt-out trucks on the road to Jerusalem

The Sorek Stalagmite Cave in Absalom's Reserve

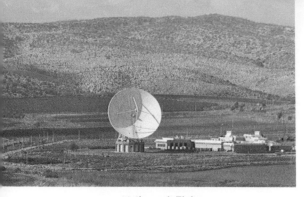
Valley of Elah

The caves at Beit Gibrin

Ramle, the famous White Tower

frequented way turns left from the tree-nursery village of **Eshtaol** to **Kibbutz Zorah,** the environs of which were the territory originally allotted to the tribe of Dan — "Zorah, and Eshtaol, and Ir-shemesh." (Joshua 19:41). Samson was a Danite, and Judges 16:31 relates that, after his death among the Philistines, his family "buried him between Zorah and Eshtaol."

Beit Shemesh, the House of the Sun, known in the book of Joshua as Ir-shemesh, the Town of the Sun, is today an urban and industrial centre of some 11,000 people, established in 1950, with a number of important factories. Ancient Beit Shemesh was a major city during the Canaanite era, and again during First Temple times. After the division of the kingdom following Solomon's death, the border towns were fortified, and II Kings 14:11 records how "Jehoash king of Israel... and Amaziah king of Judah looked one another in the face at Beth-shemesh, which belongeth to Judah." Jehoash killed Amaziah there, in Beit Shemesh, and went on to attack Jerusalem.

Incidentally, routine quarrying operations carried out in the Beit Shemesh district in 1967 opened up one of the most extraordinary caverns ever discovered in the Mediterranean region, Sorek Cave in Absalom's Reserve. Although small in size, covering only about 5 dunams (1¼ acres) it is incredibly rich in stalactite, stalagmite and filmy travertine formations. It is now within the boundaries of the American Bicentennial Park of the Jewish National Fund, and is cared for by the Nature Reserves Authority.

The **Adullam Region** was planned on a satellite system of agricultural villages grouped around a hub providing schools, clinics, stores and other essentials, while **Beit Gibrin,** once a stronghold of Rehoboam, king of Judah, has extensive Byzantine and Crusader remains, as well as a labyrinth of enormous caves, some with Greek inscriptions.

As you continue along the regular, direct road to Ramle, note the Italian-style **Monastery of Latrun** standing amidst groves of cypress trees and seemingly-endless vineyards. Built some 50 years ago, it houses Trappist monks who have taken a vow of silence, although one is always available to act as host and sell the monks' produce of wine, cheese and honey.

A track skirting the monastery quickly brings you to the ruins of the great third century **Church of the Maccabees** — the earliest church so far discovered — where pillar capitals inscribed in Hebrew and Greek were found. Some authorities believe that this village, Amwas, one of the battlefields of the Maccabees, was the true Emmaus, where the resurrected Jesus was invited by Cleophas and Simon to "Abide with us, for the day is far spent," while others place Emmaus at el-Qubeibe. On the hill above, the Crusader castle of **Les Toron des Chevaliers** still protects the defile through the Valley of Ayalon.

On your left is **Tel Gezer,** among the most important mounds in the country, for not only was it situated between the plain and the foothills, but it stood on a rise on the ancient Via Maris and opened the way up to Jerusalem. Excavated for the Palestine Exploration Fund by R.A. Macalister in 1902, the dig was recently renewed by Dr. Frank Deever of the Hebrew Union College. The earlier

dig found walls and towers of the finest type of Canaanite construction; a 200 feet water tunnel; the famous "High Place," with ten standing stones, and the tenth century BCE Calendar Stone, written in archaic Hebrew and listing the farmer's duties for each month of the year.

Although "Horam king of Gezer came to help Lachish; and Joshua smote him and his people," (Joshua 10:33), you later read in I Kings 9:16 that "Pharoah, king of Egypt, had gone up and taken Gezer... and given it for a present unto his daughter, Solomon's wife." Solomon restored Gezer, and part of his monumental architecture was unearthed not long ago.

At Ramle junction, the road bears right to the Talmudic town of Lod. Away from the highway is **Modiin,** the native village of Hasmonean Mattathias and his five sons, with the traditional Tombs of the Maccabees. From Modiin, relay runners carry the lighted torch to the opening of the Maccabiah Games, wherever it may be held.

Lod itself, better known as **Lydda,** has a long history dating back to pre-biblical times. Today this partly new, partly old and dilapidated town of about 39,000 inhabitants has two sites worth visiting — the Cathedral of Martyred St. George, patron saint of England, and Beybars Bridge, put up in 1278 and still carrying the road

Ben Gurion International Airport, Lod

Antipatris Fortress in Afek Park, Petach Tikva

the places worthy of note is **Petach Tikva** — the Gate of Hope — where the first ever agricultural colony was established in 1878 by Jews from the Old City of Jerusalem. From small beginnings it has grown into a town of 120,000 souls. Close to it is the immigrant township of **Rosh Ha'Ayin,** with about 12,000 Yemenites who arrived in Israel in 1950.

Historic Rosh Ha'Ayin, or **Ras el-Ain,** however, is the mound guarding the headsprings of the Yarkon, the biblical Aphek, on the ancient Via Maris. Joshua 12:18 includes "the king of Aphek," in the list of the defeated kings, and I Samuel 4:1 describes how the "Philistines pitched in Aphek" before joining battle with the Israelites. Always having the connotation of abundant water, it was known as Pegai under the Greeks, and Arethusa when conquered by the Maccabees. It remained Arethusa until Herod the Great rebuilt it and called it Antipatris, after his father.

S t r a n g e l y enough, the Mishnaic period referred to the place by its Greek name, calling it Mei Piga — the Waters of Piga. In later years it was covered by a Crusader castle, then by a Turkish fort, for the 2000 springs bubbling out of the earth created one of the chief water sources of the country. In 1926 the British drew a pipeline from here to

across the Wadi Ayalon. The perfectly preserved Arabic inscription recalls the deeds of the Mameluke slave-sultan, Beybars, the scourge of the Crusaders.

At present, however, Lod's paramount importance for Israel is its **Ben Gurion International Airport,** which not only transports tremendous air traffic to and from all parts of the world, but has maintenance and repair shops capable of tackling the most complicated procedures.

North from Lydda extends the heavily settled Sharon Plain, where among

Petach Tikva, partial view

Rishon Lezion Wine Cellars

Jerusalem, and in 1955, another was installed to bring water to the arid Negev. At the present time a systematic excavation is being carried out on the site by Dr. M. Kochavi, and has already produced remarkable results.

Back in **Ramle,** take note that it was built in 717 CE, the only town ever established by the Arabs in Palestine. Later fortified by the Crusaders, it is at present a busy, go-ahead market town, with a population of around 33,000, of whom 4000 are non-Jews. The White Tower — a conspicuous landmark — is part of the fourteenth century White Mosque, while other places to see in Ramle are the eighth century Cisterns of St. Helena, and the Crusader Cathedral, now the Great Mosque.

South of Ramle is the famous old-established **Rishon Lezion,** started with the help of the Rothschild family in 1882. One of the large wine-producing centres of Israel, it has over 92,000 inhabitants. **Rehovot,** another early colony dating from 1890, is the centre of Israel's citrus industry, with a population of around 67,000. What distinguishes Rehovot from other towns, however, is the academy of higher learning called the **Weizman Institute of Science** founded in 1934 by the late president Dr. Haim Weizman.

Begun on a small scale in 1891 with the inception of an Agricultural Experimental Station, it is now a large complex, with the most modern architecture and up-to-date, sophisticated equipment. Some 500 scientists are on the staff, and about the same number of postgraduate students study there for their Doctorates and Masters degrees.

The scope of the work done at the Institute is widespread, encompassing many aspects of organic and physical chemistry, nuclear physics, biophysics and biochemistry, computor specialization, genetics and a host of other fields. Emphasis is placed on research.

The Weizman Institute is set in carefully tended gardens with green lawns, flower beds, trees and shrubs, while the archives and library are open to the public. Visitors can also see Dr. Weizman's house, now a museum, and may pause for a moment at the tree-shaded tomb of Dr. Weizman and his wife Vera, who are buried in the compound.

The Tombs of Chaim and Vera Weizman

The Weizman Institute, Rehovot

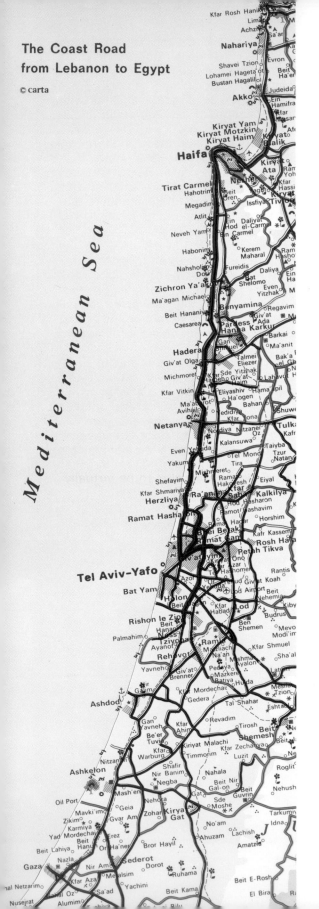

The Coast Road
from Lebanon to Egypt

© carta

Mediterranean Sea

"The west border was to the Great Sea, and the coast thereof." Joshua 15:12.

ISRAEL'S COAST, running south from **Rosh Ha'Nikra** — the Ladder of Tyre — to the sandy wastes of Northern Sinai is, generally speaking, a smooth stretch of the Mediterranean's eastern shore. Its only real indentation of harbour size is the Haifa — Acre bay, otherwise the shoreline is mostly one of sandy beaches and sheltered coves.

At its northernmost point, bordering on Lebanon, are the Rosh Ha'Nikra grottoes, where the railway used to pass through a rock-cut tunnel, and where today the waves churn and roar through rock caverns and subterranean passages. A little further south is **Nahariya,** a pleasant seaside town of some 22,000 inhabitants, with the Gaaton Brook flowing through its main street. Founded in 1934 by immigrants from Nazi-dominated Germany, it soon became an orderly, efficient community of small-holders and hotel keepers.

Rosh Ha'Nikra, the cliffs

Nahariya, Gaaton Avenue

Achziv and the Ladder of Tyre

Kibbutz Lohamei Hageta'ot is located directly off the road joining Nahariya to Acre, and adjoins a section of the Turkish aqueduct which once brought water from the Springs of Ķabri to the town of Acre. Established in April 1949 by survivors of the European holocaust, Kibbutz Lohamei Hageta'ot commemorates the defenders of the Warsaw Ghetto, and its museum recalls by documents, photographs and mechanical models the heroic resistance of the Jewish ghettoes of Europe during World War II.

When Joshua entered Canaan and divided it up among the children of Israel, **Acre** and its surroundings fell to the lot of Asher. However, Judges 1: 31 tells that, "Neither did Asher drive out the inhabitants of Accho, but the Asherites dwelt among the Canaan - ites, the inhabitants of the land." A seaport from very ancient times, it was on the Via Maris and had connections with the cross-country highway to the east, and the Way of the Patriarchs, linking Egypt to the empires of the north. First mentioned 4000 years ago in the Egyptian Execration Texts, then in the Amarna letters and other documents of the fifteenth to

the thirteenth centuries BCE, it continued to be referred to as a prosperous harbour town through the ages. In 333 BCE, Acre opened its gates to Alexander of Macedon, and was rewarded by permission to be virtually independent and to mint its own coins. Renamed Ptolemais, it continued to thrive, although neither the Hasmoneans nor the Herodians managed to annex it to their kingdoms. Under the Romans it became the army headquarters, and from here as-

Ghetto Fighters' House and the Aqueduct

saults were launched on the Jewish strongholds of Galilee.

The Moslems took the town in 636 CE, and reverted to the use of its ancient name; then the Crusaders in 1104 made Acre their chief port, setting up the Kingdom of Acre, which lasted until 1291. Destroyed by the Mamelukes, the city of Acre began to pick up only in the seventeenth century, and in 1775 Ahmed el-Jazzar, known as the Butcher, for his extreme cruelty, erected the Great Mosque with marble columns shipped in from Ashkelon and Caesarea. He also built the Hammam — the Baths — now the Municipal Museum, the Khan of the Pillars, and the aqueduct bringing water from the springs of **Kabri.**

With the help of the British, Jazzar staved off Napoleon's two-month siege of Acre in 1799, but by 1840, the town was again under the Turks. In 1918 it was included in the British Mandate, and in 1948, with the Declaration of Independence, Acre began to develop rapidly.

Now a lively town of some 40,000 people, about a quarter of them non-Jews, Acre combines up-to-date services with mediaeval grace. Its mos-ques and minarets; its khans; its covered markets; its museums, the Sea Wall and moat, built on Crusader foundations, and the Land Gate are all worth seeing. More and more of the grandiose Crusader structures, like the Crypt of St. John, are gradually being revealed, and a special visit should be paid to the eighteenth century Citadel, used as a prison, where the British held and often executed Jewish freedom fighters. Part of it is today a mental hospital.

Haifa, on the opposite point of the bay, is a modern harbour able to accommodate all sizes of luxury liners, tankers, cargo boats and other ships. Along the quays are grain silos; warehouses; a container terminal; repair shops and all the facilities needed for equipping every kind of vessel. Giant vats mark the Haifa refineries, once the terminal of the Irak oil pipeline, and now utilized for Israel's own requirements. Wide shady roads climb the hills behind the town to attractive suburbs, where building is going on apace, and the Technion and the Haifa University are turning out highly-qualified engineers and scholars in every field.

Aerial view of Acre from the south

St. John's Crypt

The Fishermen's Harbour

Ideally situated as it is, between the sea and forested Mount Carmel, of which Isaiah 35:2 says, "the excellency of Carmel," the environs of Haifa have been a favourite habitation for untold generations. Prehistoric man lived here in the caves of Carmel and, before the coming of the Israelites, there were Phoenicians at Shikmona, on the coast directly south of Haifa, and to the north-west, near the present suburb of Bat Galim. There were fishermen, who also produced the famous Royal Purple dye from the murex snails found locally and, it is said, introduced the craft of glass-making with the fine silica sand on the shore.

During the Talmudic period, Haifa was overwhelmingly Jewish, famed for its

The Bahai Shrine in the Persian Gardens, Haifa

Haifa, view from Mount Carmel

scholars, sailors and craftsmen and, together with the Arabs who had come in with the invasion of 636, they unsuccessfully tried to resist the Crusader troops. Wrested from the Crusaders and destroyed by the Mamelukes in 1265, Haifa remained an insignificant colony for 500 years. Beginning with slow growth, Haifa progressed by leaps and bounds after World War I, when the British made full use of the port, and since the War of Independence, it has never looked back.

Dominating Haifa's landscape from the sea is the golden dome of the **Bahai Temple.** Set in formal gardens is the grave of the Persian-born Bab — the Gate, or the Forerunner — who was executed in 1850 at the age of 31, for his religious teachings. The principles of the Bahai faith were formulated by his prophet, Baha'ullah, who was imprisoned by the Turks in Acre Citadel. He died in Acre in 1892, and his tomb on the northern outskirts of the town is perhaps the most sacred of the Bahai shrines.

Introduced in 1844 by the Bab as the newest of the New Revelations of the Divinity, the Bahai faith stresses the unity of God and the brotherhood of Mankind. A seemingly undemanding religion, the Bahai belief has attracted more than a million adherents from all over the world, notably from England and the United States; India; Africa; Iran, the Philippines and others. Although their World Centre is here, as is their Council House, Library and Archives, there are few local believers. Those who live here are barely 100, among them the nine members of the Bahai Supreme Council.

Besides the Bahai shrines, Haifa has a number of outstanding museums, including the Maritime Museum, the Museum of Ethnology, the Dagon Grain Museum, and that of Japanese Art. On the outskirts, at **Mukhraka,** is Elijah's altar, marked by a Carmelite monastery standing where "Elijah went up to the top of Carmel," (I Kings 18:42), and slew the false prophets of Baal.

Daliyat el-Carmel, a Druze village

Mt. Carmel Mukhraka, Elijah's monument

A short excursion should be taken from Haifa to **Beit Shearim,** where there is a rock-hewn necropolis of the second century CE. Here were buried some of the foremost scholars of the period, while carved sarcophagi and inscriptions in Hebrew, Aramaic and Greek, tell a story of their own. Here are the ruins, too, of a Second Temple town, with streets and houses; a synagogue; flour mills, olive presses and a wine-press.

Another side journey is to **Daliyat el-Carmel,** one of the 16 Druze villages in the Carmel and Galilee. Daliyat el-Carmel is a little different from the others, for it has a busy market of Druze folkcraft, and was also the home of the nineteenth century British Christian Zionist, Laurence Oliphant, and his lovely wife, Alice. Their home is still here.

The **Druze** are an unusual people, whose faith branched off from Islam around 1000 CE, and has since then kept apart. No converts are accepted; they marry only among their own faith, and they have stayed for centuries on the land tilled by their forefathers. Altogether there are about 300,000 Druze, the majority in Syria and Lebanon. Thirty-three thousand live in Israel as loyal subjects of the State, serving in the army, in the Border Police and in government offices. Jethro, Moses' father-in-law, is the Druze prophet. His grave is at Nebi Shueib, near the Horns of Hittin,

Beit Shearim, the burial cave

Bird's eye view of Zichron Ya'acov

Views of Netanya

where his followers gather annually on 25th April.

The Castle of Atlit — Castrum Peregrinorum, or Pilgrims' Castle — was built around 1220 expressly for Christian pilgrims who docked their small boats at the haven of Atlit. Walls, a refectory, stores and a church can still be seen, while more modern remains are those of the Rothschild-sponsored salt factory, now disused, and the experimental agricultural station of Aaron Aaronson, head of the Nili spy ring aiding the British in World War I.

Dor, or Dora, the present-day Tantura, was an important, already ancient port when Joshua invaded the Promised Land and fought the local chieftains, of whom one was "the king of Dor in the coast of Dor" (Joshua 12:23). One of Solomon's officers over his twelve food-producing districts was the son of Abinadab, who administered "all the region of Dor"

The restored Roman theatre at Caesarea

Natanya, the famous Mediterranean sea-shore resort

(I Kings 4:11). Dor continued to flourish under Greek, Hasmonean and Roman rule, and the colossal, formless masses of ruins on the shore are witness to Dor's glorious past. Today, **Kibbutz Nachsholim** runs a Guest House there, as well as a restaurant and bathing beach.

Israel's foremost wineproducing centre is the wooded Carmel townlet of **Zichron Ya'acov**, founded in 1882 and named in honour of James de Rothschild, who did so much for Palestine in the early days. His mausoleum at Ramat Ha'Nadiv is worth a visit, so are the wine-cellars and the Aaronson House Museum, with its touching memories of Sara Aaronson and the tragedy played out within its walls.

Against the glittering background of the sea rises the restored Crusader city of **Caesarea,** with its moat and battlements, its vaulted halls, churches, flag-stoned street, cisterns and dwellings. This was but one chapter in the long annals of Caesarea, cons-

tructed by Herod in 20 BCE on the site of the Phoenician anchorage of Straton's Tower, and named for Augustus Caesar. Josephus tells in his Antiquities, book 15:9, that Herod "erected edifices of white stone and sumptuous palaces... also a theatre of stone and, on the south, an amphitheatre." This same amphitheatre, cleared and renovated, is now used for the Summer Festival of concerts and plays.

For 600 years Caesarea was the capital of the Roman province of Judea which, at most times, held a prosperous Jewish community. From here Paul (then still known as Saul) was sent on his missions abroad, and Acts 9:30 relates how he was "brought down to Caesarea, and sent to Tarsus." He was imprisoned in Caesarea, then, when "King Agrippa and Bernice came unto Caesarea." (Acts 25:13), he talked with them. Here, in 66 CE, began the Jewish revolt against the Romans and here, at the end of Bar Kochba's rebellion, Rabbi Akiba was tortured and killed by the Romans. Christianity quickly gained ground in Caesarea, and Christian scholars like Origen and Eusebius lived there in the third and fourth centuries CE side by side with Talmudic sages. After a bitter struggle, Caesarea fell to the Moslems in 646, but they kept it well. "Its milk and white bread are famous," wrote a tenth century geographer about Caesarea, "and its fruit delicious." Rebuilt as a Crusader citadel-town of some 50 acres, less than a tenth of the Herodian city, it prospered until it was vanquished by the Mameluke sultan Beybars in 1291, and was virtually abandoned.

Only in 1940 did Caesarea begin to revive, when **Kibbutz Sdot Yam** was founded in the south, with a Guest House and a museum of local finds. In 1951 the immigrant town of **Or Akiba,** named for martyred Rabbi Akiba, was set up, then a five-star hotel, a golf course and luxury villas followed, contributing to the awakening of Caesarea. Tourists from Israel and abroad come in their thousands to see the Herodian amphitheatre, hippodrome and other remains, the Byzantine market place and statues, and the restored Crusader fortress, as well as to enjoy the golden beaches and bays of Caesarea's sea coast.

Natanya is geared both for vacationing and permanent living, and has become the most popular place in Israel for the middle-class European tourist and for English-speaking immigrants. Founded in 1928 and named for the American philanthropist, Nathan Strauss, it rapidly developed into a holiday and industrial town of over 100,000 citizens. There are beautiful beaches; cliff walks; public gardens, entertainment and a modern amphitheatre as well as a wide choice of good hotels and restaurants. In the commercial field, it has become the centre of Israel's important diamond industry.

Herzlia, too, is a popular resort with excellent hotels, while some of its residential suburbs are among the finest to be found anywhere. On the seashore is **Apollonia,** called Arsuf in Canaanite times and Rishpon in the days of the kings of Israel. Overrun by the Assyrians when Israel fell, it was rebuilt during Greek domination as Apollonia, while under the Crusaders it was again Arsuf. Close to its ruins is the Mosque of Sidna Ali, a Moslem commander in the Mameluke army.

Tel Aviv-Jaffa is an old-new city, a metropolis with a population of about 334,000 — second largest in Israel. Although under a single administration, there is no comparison between Tel Aviv and Jaffa. **Tel Aviv** is a modern

Tel Aviv, sea front

Dizengoff square, Fire-Water Sculpture by Y. Agam

town, established by 60 families in 1909 as Ahuzat Bayit, an all-Jewish village of homes and gardens not far from Jaffa. It suffered a severe setback during World War I, when the Turks expelled the Jews and sent them inland, but when General Allenby rode in in 1918, the exiles streamed back and were quickly reinforced by floods of immigrants.

Israel's commercial and cultural centre, Tel Aviv boasts shops of international standards, the Mann Auditorium, the Habima and additional smaller theatres, and a host of exhibition halls and museums. Among the museums is the Museum Ha'aretz complex near Tel Qasile, once a busy Philistine town and trading post; the Haganah Museum, the Tel Aviv Museum and Wax Work Museum. The newest attraction is Beit Hatefutzot — the Diaspora Museum. Especially popular with children are the Ramat Gan Safari Park and the Dolphinarium, where dolphins frolic and perform tricks to the delight of the onlookers!

Tel Aviv's fast-growing University Campus is constantly adding new buildings and faculties, as is the Bar Ilan University in Ramat Gan, with its orthodox background. Allenby Street's Great Synagogue is one of the largest in the country.

Jaffa — biblical Joppa — is quite different. Legends hold that its founder was Japhet, son of Noah, and even documentary evidence goes back 3500 years, to the time when the Egyptian monarch, Thuthmos III, peacefully entered the town in 1468 BCE, fetching in with him hundreds of soldiers in innocent-looking hampers. The second book of Chronicles 2:16 tells how Solomon discussed his building projects with Hiram, king of Tyre, who said, "We will cut wood out of Lebanon... and bring it in floats by sea to Joppa," for this was Israel's outlet to the wide world. Jonah 1:3, relates how he "went down to Joppa, and he found a ship going to Tarshish," while Christians associate Jaffa with Peter, who restored Tabitha to life and "tarried many days with one Simon, a tanner," (Acts 9:43).

A tourist today can spend some time in Jaffa seeing the Artists' Quarter, with its quaint streets and workshops; the Museum of Archaeology and the dig beside it; St. Peter's Church and the House of Simon the Tanner, the Clock Tower and the Flea Market — a paradise for bargain hunters.

Just south of Jaffa lies **Bat Yam,** one of the nicest holiday resorts in the centre of Israel. A fast growing town with over 140,000 inhabitants, Bat

Tel Aviv-Jaffa coastline, with ancient Jaffa in the foreground

The Church of St. Peter, Jaffa

Yam has beautiful beaches and a gay night-life and is ideally situated for touring the country.

As Jaffa is Israel's oldest port, so **Ashdod** — the New Testament Azotus — is its newest. Built in 1957 chiefly for the export of citrus, it has quickly become an important business area of over 65,000 people, with dock facilities, an electric power station, and a recently opened container terminal. Nearby is the site of Old Testament Ashdod (Joshua 15:47), one of the five major Philistine cities. "The Philistines took the ark of God, and brought it from Ebenezer unto Ashdod," you read in I Samuel 5:1, and there "they brought it into the house of Dagon," with disastrous consequences.

Ashkelon has pleasanter memories. A residential and vacation town of 54,000 people, it has made good use of the archaeological fragments unearthed in the Palestine Exploration Fund's dig of 1920 to 1921. One of the oldest and largest cities in this part of the world, Ashkelon was, 4000 years ago, a Canaanite city-state under Egyptian protection. Later, together with Ashdod, Ekron, Gath and Gaza, it became one of the five chief Philistine towns interwoven with the actions of the Israelites as recorded in the book of Judges, and particularly with the wanderings of the Holy Ark.

Under Greek domination, Ashkelon was an independent city, possibly the birthplace of Herod the Great. When he came to power, he built palatial buildings and colonnaded walks there, adding statues and fountains. Ashkelon thrived during Roman and Byzantine days — a large synagogue from this time has been discovered — and it became one of the key coastal fortresses of the Crusaders. Ashkelon followed the same, unhappy pattern as the rest of the Crusader strongholds, for it was razed by Beybars in 1270, and lay ruined for centuries. Many of the columns, capitals and statues of ancient Ashkelon were placed in the National Park there, while in **Barnea** to the north, on the seashore, is a Byzantine decorative mosaic church floor.

Negba, then the most southerly kibbutz in Palestine, played an outstanding role in throwing back the Egypt-

The modern town and harbour of Ashdod

The beach at Bat Yam

ians in 1948, and the Negba War Memorial has become a symbol of bravery. **Yad Mordechai,** a kibbutz established in 1943 and named for Mordechai Anilewitz, leader of the Warsaw ghetto rising, was actually taken by the Egyptians and later retaken by the Israelis. Life-size models depict the fateful 1948 battle.

Before 1967 **Gaza,** once one of the five great Philistine towns, was on the Egyptian side of the Green Line. An ancient city on the timeless Via Maris, it was both a sea and a land junction, from where roads ran north to the cultivated areas; east to Beersheba, Transjordan, and the Nabatean towns, and a place where the caravans could stock up with all they needed before journeying south through the Sinai desert.

Gaza continued to be an important seaport throughout history. Part of Herod's kingdom, it became especially prosperous with the flourishing of the Nabatean states, and on into Byzantine times, when Jewish communities lived there. At least two elaborate mosaic synagogue floors of this period were found in Gaza, and in the mosque, previously a Crusader church, is a pillar bearing a menorah and a Hebrew and Greek inscription. During World War I, Gaza was besieged by British troops for nearly a year, and was eventually taken only after a heavy loss of life.

In 1948 Egypt annexed Gaza and the Gaza Strip, which measures scarcely 30 by 4 miles, and was packed with nearly 400,000 refugees and others.

After the Six Day War Israel tried to alleviate Gaza's dreadful conditions, providing more work, improved housing and medical services, simultaneously setting up a string of settlements southward along the coast. With the return of Sinai to Egypt in April 1982, all those flourishing communities — Dikla, Sadot, Nahal Sinai and others —including the model townlet of Yamit, have had to be abandoned as part of the price of peace.

Ashkelon, ancient ruins at the National Park

Yad Mordechai, the M. Anilewitz Memorial

Nof Katif vacation village

"And Abram journeyed, going on still toward the south."

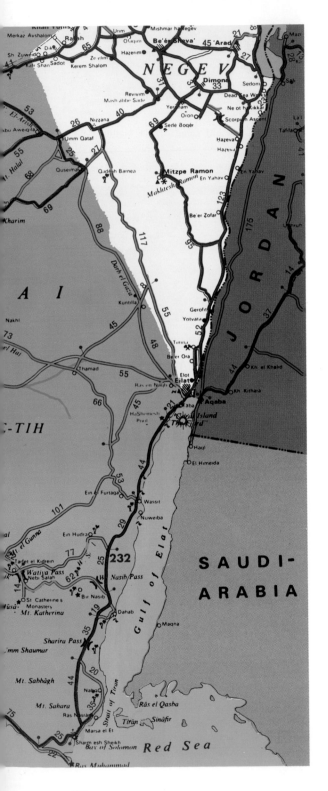

SOUTH FROM BEERSHEBA stretches the bleak semi-desert of the Negev, gradually being restored to life and productivity. One of the most encouraging places to visit there is **Kibbutz Sde Boker,** where David Ben Gurion made his modest home in 1953, a year after the inauguration of the kibbutz. Here he planned a great future for the Negev — a future of agricultural and industrial development.

Much has come to fruition. Sde Boker itself is flourishing, and has attached to it the Sde Boker Academy (Midrasha), a Field School and Regional High School. David Ben Gurion and Paula his wife were buried here, and their twin graves attract a constant stream of people who come to pay homage to a great man, a true Founding Father of the State of Israel.

Close to Sde Boker, an observation

The tombs of Paula and David Ben-Gurion at Sde Boker

platform affords a remarkable view down the **Avdat Canyon.** A walk through the canyon is an experience. You start off between sheer white cliffs, the ravine narrowing as it approaches Ein Avdat, a deep, translucent pool of icy water, fed by a small waterfall. Further on is Ein Mor — the Bitter Pool — with a high salt content, and beyond is yet another.

Ein Avdat takes its name from nearby Avdat, or Oboda, one of the six Nabatean towns in the vicinity, the others being Mamshit (Kurnub), Shivta (Subeita), Nitzana (Nessana), Halutza (Elusa), and Rehovot b'Negev, or Rubeiba. The **Nabateans** were a trading nation who had their beginnings around the third century BCE, and over the years grew in power and importance by controlling the caravan routes. These routes linked Gaza on the Mediterranean to Elath on the Red Sea, extended across to Arabia, transporting perfumes and spices, and up through Jerusalem to the lands of the north.

Their capital was the "rose-red city" of Petra, now in Jordan, and they were most influential between the second century BCE and the first century CE, when the Romans changed their status from that of an empire into a Roman province. However, the Nabateans retained their culture, their characteristic architecture and handicraft, and later appear to have been Christianized and absorbed into the Byzantine regime. The basilicas you see on the Nabatean sites are late additions.

Avdat, first of the Nabatean towns to be restored, is typical in its town planning, with paved streets draining into communal cisterns; well-built houses, and other communal facilities such as those for wine-making, pottery-firing and so on. Their system of water collection and storage was remarkable, making the Negev blossom; and experiments to copy their methods have been in progress near Avdat since the 1950's. An interesting sidelight is the fact that all early inscriptions found on Nabatean sites were in Aramaic, a language very similar to Hebrew.

Ben Gurion's Hut, Kibbutz Sde Boker

The Desert of Zin in the Negev

The ancient ruins at Avdat

Bird's eye view of Avdat

Mizpeh Ramon and the Ramon crater

Shivta and Mamshit have also been restored, but Nitzana, Halutza and Rehovot b'Negev have been revived by proxy in neighbouring **Kibbutz Revivim,** or Dewdrops, one of the first three agricultural settlements initiated in the Negev in 1943.

Not far from Nitzana, is biblical **Kadesh Barnea,** a good-sized oasis and the cross-roads of the ancient world. It was probably a semi-permanent camp of the children of Israel in their journey through the wilderness, for Numbers 13:26 relates how the twelve spies "returned after forty days; and they went to Moses... in Kadesh," while another reference is to the children of Israel who came

and "abode in Kadesh, and Miriam died there and was buried there," (Numbers 20:1).

Archaeological finds here include a large First Monarchy fortress on Davidic foundations, while there are al-

so traces of Edomite, Nabatean and Byzantine occupation. This is not surprising, for the springs are rich, **Ein Qudeirat** alone producing 40 cubic metres an hour. C.S. Jarvis, the British governor of Sinai during the Mandate, cleared the well for the use of the local Bedouin.

On the Arava road linking Sdom to Elath, you pass the oasis of **Ein Husub,** where the new settlement of **Hatzeva** jostles the remnants of a Roman fort. Further south is **Ein Yahav,** then **Ketura,** manned by an American youth movement, and **Grofit,** a Kibbutz with urban-style building surrounded by fruitful fields. **Yotvata** was founded in 1951 on the freshwater springs of Ein Radian, which always supplied water to Elath. Here are remains of an Israelite citadel, a Roman guard tower, and a British military outpost.

Close by is the Hai Bar biblical wild life reserve where, in an area of 8000

Hai Bar wild life reserve near Elath

King Solomon's Pillars

acres of semi-desert, a successful attempt is being made to restore to this land creatures which roamed here in biblical times. Opened in 1977 the Hai-Bar Reserve now houses various horned animals such as the Oryx, the Addax, the Ibex and the Gazelle.

Also there are the Ostrich, the Wild Ass and many nocturnal fauna like wolves, hyaenas, foxes and the Desert Lynx.

Timna copper mines have produced copper, on and off, for 6000 years. Unfounded tales associate the Timna mines with Solomon, but excavations carried out by Dr. Beno Rothenberg from 1959 to 1969 paint a different picture. Timna was the earliest copper mine in the world, for it was efficiently utilized in 4000 BCE, while in the fifteenth century BCE it became an important Egyptian industry. In the shadow of the huge rocks known as **Solomon's Pillars,** Dr. Rothenberg

discovered an Egyptian temple to the goddess Hathor, together with over 11,000 inscriptions. A Midianite shrine of about 1250 BCE — the time of Moses — was also found, and in it

The Timna Lake

153

The Timna Park

were various statuettes, notably that of a copper snake, reminiscent of Numbers 21:9, in which you read, "Moses made a serpent of brass, and put it upon a pole." Abandoned for over 1000 years, the copper mines were re-used by the Romans until the third century CE, then they were neglected until modern times.

A new Nature Reserve — Timna Park sponsored by Kibbutz Elot has recently been opened. In addition to awe-inspiring scenery, it includes part of the ancient copper mines ; an excavated Temple of Hathor, and the stone "Mushroom".

A side track just before Elath leads to **Amram's Pillars,** a striking rock formation of red and bluish sandstone named for Moses' father. Soon you reach **Elath,** at the head of the Gulf of Elath opening into the Red Sea.

A town which has passed through many vicissitudes, Elath is first mentio-

The Coral World Underwater Observatory and Aquarium

ned in Numbers 33:35, which tells how the children of Israel, on their way to Kadesh Barnea around 3300 years ago, "encamped in Ezion-ga-ber" while I Kings 9:26 describes how "Solomon made a navy for ships at Ezion-Gaber which is beside Eloth."

Called Berenice by the Egyptian Pto-lemies, it was renamed Aila by the Romans, and it continued to thrive under the Byzantines, the early Arabs and the Crusaders.

Abandoned after the second Moslem invasion, it contained nothing but a derelict police post called Um Rash-rash — still to be seen near the Red Rock Hotel — when the Israel Defen-ce Army took Elath in March 1949. It started off slowly. Distances from the country's population centres were great — it was 200 miles to Jeru-salem, 225 to Tel Aviv and 300 to Haifa. Roads were poor or non-exis-tent, and interurban air travel in its infancy.

The year 1956 saw Elath at a low ebb, with 500 people and few prospects; but after the Sinai Campaign in Octo-ber 1956, the town began to develop. A highway to the rest of the country was initiated; daily flights to all the main centres were started, while port facilities were enlarged and included a special section for oil handling. Pro-gress continued, but it was the Six Day War of June 1967 which really inaugurated a new era of expansion for Elath.

Instead of being a cul-de-sac, it be-came the springboard to the Sinai Peninsula — an enormous land mass of untamed natural beauty and histo-rical significance, honeycombed with Moslem pilgrim routes going to and from Mecca. Israel's control of Sinai lasted until April 1982, during which time tremendous strides were made in the hitherto neglected and undeveloped territory.

A road edging the shore from Elath to Sharm-el-Sheikh was laid; water and electricity lines were brought in and new oil wells discovered and activated. Airfields were built, and seaside vacation resorts like Neviot, Di-zahav and Na'ama sprang up, of-fering various kinds of accommoda-tion, sailing, swimming, diving, and water sports.

Sharm-el-Sheikh, renamed Ophira, at the southern tip of the peninsula, quickly became a lively holiday town and the urban district centre for the area.

Although the Sinai Peninsula is now

Underwater scenery in the Red Sea

The Red Canyon

View from Eilat to Akaba

again under Egyptian jurisdiction, the 15-year period of the Elath-Sinai ambience made a deep, positive impression on the Red Sea town. With a population of over 20,000, it has today full employment, good housing and travel facilities, schools, a hospital and other health services. The recently completed man-made lagoon, circled by top-level hotels, is an important tourist attraction, while there is an abundance of less luxurious hotels, of pensions, hostels and camping sites.

Apart from its incredible all-the-year-round summer and constant sun shine, Elath is a convenient base for trips into the Negev, to Timna, to the Hai-Bar Nature Reserve and other places of interest. It also offers the widest range possible of water sports of every kind, and has excellent fish restaurants and discos as well as a remarkable underwater observatory, one of only four similar structures in the world.

Opened in 1974, it became instantly popular. The complex consists of a museum, 24 aquaria displaying rare and striking sea creatures, and a large tank for sharks and outsize specimens. Then a 100-yard long pier leads out to an underwater observation chamber from which can be seen a kaleidoscope of colourful tropical fish, corals and waterplants. Not only is Elath a favourite resort for Israelis, but it has become a playground paradise for sun-hungry European tourists. Package tours offering charter flights from Europe, a stay at a 5-star hotel plus several excursions have become tremendouly popular, and have added considerably to Elath's economic development.

Until April 1982, Elath and Sinai were a single entity, and both Israelis and foreign visitors streamed southwards to enjoy the sights and wonders of the desert peninsula. One of the outstanding sites is Jebel Mussa, — the Mount of Moses, or Mount Sinai — where, tradition holds, Moses received the Tablets of the Law. Exodus 19:20 graphically describes how "the Lord came down upon Mount Sinai... and called Moses up to the top of the Mount; and Moses went up."

At the foot of the mountain is the Greek Orthodox Monastery of St. Catherine, a martyred fourth century saint, erected on the traditional site of Moses' Burning Bush, Here Moses heard the voice of the Lord from a bush which "burned with fire, and was not consumed. (Exodus 3:2).

Perhaps the most impressive structure of this kind in the whole of the Middle East, the great fortified monastery was built by Emperor Justinian in the sixth century, and a Greek inscription there dedicates it to him and his wife Theodora.

Particular points of interest are the Cathedral of the Transfiguration, with a fine wall mosaic, which is probably the oldest of the buildings; the Charnel House of the deceased monks, and the library, with a wealth of rare icons and manuscripts.

Another noteworthy spot is Serabit el-Khadem, with remains of ancient turquoise mines and of a temple to the Egyptian goddess Hathor. A number of stelae, inscribed with hieroglyphics and Proto-Sinaitic script are still in place. Spectacular scenery can be found in the colourful oases of Wadi Firan, of Sin Hudra and Ein Furtuga.

Wind Surfing on the Red Sea

The handing over of Sinai to Egypt is one of the great concessions made by Israel in return for a lasting peace with her southern neighbour. At the moment there is a border post between the two countries at a point just south of Elath, but Israelis are wholeheartedly looking forward to the mutual goodwill and prosperity which will be brought about by free access from both sides — the forerunner of real peace, progress and understanding.

The Marina at Elath

Fig   **Dates**   **Wheat**   **Pomegranates**

a land of wheat, and barley, and vines, and fig trees, and pomegranates; a land of olive oil and honey. (Deut. 8, 7-8)

Olives   **Grapes**   **Barley**

Narcissus	Negev Iris	Sea Squill	Crown Daisy

FLOWERS OF ISRAEL

Common Anemone   Colchicum steveni   Cyclamen

PEOPLE OF ISRAEL

NOTES

NOTES

NOTES

NOTES

CHRONOLOGICAL TABLE

1950 B.C.E.	Abraham arrived in Canaan
1350 B.C.E.	Exodus from Egypt
1250 B.C.E.	Joshua led the Children of Israel into the Promised Land
1200-1030	Time of the Judges, Deborah, Gideon, Samson etc.
1030 B.C.E.	Saul crowned King of Israel
1011-972	Reign of King David
965-922	Reign of King Solomon, Temple built
953-933	Division of kingdom into Israel and Judah —
933-722	Kings of Israel
721 B.C.E.	Samaria and Northern Kingdom destroyed
587 B.C.E.	Jerusalem and Temple destroyed by Nebuchadnezzar; Tribe of Judah exiled to Babylon
539 B.C.E.	Jews returned to Jerusalem and Temple rebuilt in 520
445 B.C.E.	Return to Zion under Ezra and Nehemiah
332	Conquest of Palestine by Alexander the Great
332-168	Hellenistic Period
167 B.C.E.	Maccabean (Hasmonean) Revolt
64 B.C.E.	Palestine conquered by Pompey
37-4 B.C.E.	Reign of Herod the Great
4-1 C.E.	Birth of Jesus
30 C.E.	Crucifixion of Jesus
66-70 C.E.	Zealots' Revolt against Rome
70 C.E.	Revolt crushed by Titus and Temple destroyed
73 C.E.	Capture of Masada, last Jewish stronghold
132-135	Bar Kochba's Revolt crushed by Hadrian
395-638	Byzantine Rule
614	Persian conquest of Palestine
638-1099	Arab-Moslem Rule
1099-1291	Crusader Period
1250-1516	Rule of the Moslem Mamelukes
1516	Palestine conquered by Turkish Ottoman Empire
1917	Palestine taken by Allies in World War I under General Allenby Balfour Declaration
1922	British Mandate
1948 (15 May)	Proclamation of the State of Israel
1956	Sinai Campaign
1967 (June)	Six Day War
1973 (October)	Yom Kippur War
1977 (Nov.)	President Sadat of Egypt visited Israel
1979 (March)	Signing of Peace Treaty with Egypt
1982 (April)	Final withdrawal from Sinai
1982 (June)	Peace for the Galilee Campaign

INDEX

Abu Ghosh	133	Ebal, Mount	99	Kennedy Memorial	63-64
Acre	7, 139-40	Ein Bokek	87	Kidron Valley	40
Adullam	134	Ein Feshka	82	Knesset	51
Afikim	94	Ein Gedi	83	Mea Shearim	50
Afula	105	Ein Gev	120	Mishkenot Shaananim	49
Ai	97	Ein Harod	93	Model of 2nd Temple	54-5
Allenby Bridge	90	Ein Qudeirat	152	Mount Herzl	55-57
Almagor	120	Ein Yahav	152	Mount Moriah	23-27
Amram's Pillars	87, 88	Elah, Valley of	134	Mount of Olives	41
Antipatris	136	Elath	154-6	Mount Ophel	38
Aphek	136	El-Jib	96	Mount Scopus	46
Apollonia	146	E-Tur	156	Mount Zion	37
Aqaba	154	Eshtaol	134	Shrine of the Book	53
Aqua Bella	133	Ezion-gaber	155	Silwan Tunnel	40
Arad	87, 88			Solomon's Quarries	22
Arava	9			Solomon's Stables	26
Arbel, Mount	113			St. Stephen's Gate	19, 21
Ashdod	6, 148			St. Peter in Gallicantu	38
Ashkelon	6, 148, 154			Temple Mount	23, 24
Atarot	97			Via Dolorosa	32
Athlit, Castle of	144	Gamla	7, 129	Western Wall	23, 26-9
Avdat	151	Gaza	6, 149	Yad ve'Shem	56-57
Ayalon, Valley of	132	Gergesa	124	Zion Gate	19, 21
Ayelet Hashachar	124	Gerizim, Mount	99-101	Jordan, River	90
Ayun Nature Reserve	126	Gezer, Tel	135		
		Gibeah	96		
		Gibeon	96, 132	Kabri	140
Banias	127	Gilboa, Mount	93	Kadesh Barnea	152
Bat Yam	148	Gilgal	90	Kazrin	130
Beatitudes, Mount of	115	Ginossar, Kibbutz	114	Ketura	152
Beersheba	76, 88	Golan Heights	7, 127-9	Kfar Blum	131
Beit Alpha	93	Gonen	131	Kfar Etzion	72
Beitsaida	119, 120	Grofit	152	Kfar Giladi	126, 130
Beit Shean	91-92			Kfar Kana	107
Beit Shearim	143			Khirbet Minyeh	114
Beit Gibrin	134	Hagoshrim	131	Kibbutz	94
Beit Zayit	133	Hai Bar Wild Life Reserve	153	Kiryat Anavim	133
Belvoir	93	Haifa	141-2	Kiryat Arba	72
Bethany	77	Hammath Gader	129	Kiryat Shmoneh	126
Beth-el	97	Hammath Tiberias	112	Kochav Hayarden	93
Bethlehem	67-70	Hatzeva	152	Korazin	116, 119, 120
Church of Nativity	68	Hazor	6, 124-5	Kuneitra	128
Rachel's Tomb	66	Hebron	6, 72-4	Kursi	121
Shepherds' Field	69	Herodion	70-71		
Beticha Valley	120	Herzlia	146		
Birket Ram	128	Horns of Hattin	108, 143	Ladder of Tyre	138
Breichat Ha'Meshushim	120	Horshat Tal	127	Latrun	132, 133, 135
Bridge of Jacob's Daughters	125	Huleh Nature Reserve	125	Lavi	108
				Lod (Lydda)	135
		Inn of the Good Samaritan	78	Lohamei Hagetaot	139
Caesarea	6, 145				
Caesarea Philippi	128			Maale Adumim	78
Capernaum	116-7	Jaffa	147	Maale Hahamisha	133
Castel, Mount	133	Jericho	6, 79-80	Magdala	113
Castle Nimrod	128	JERUSALEM	6, 7, 15-64	Mamshit	151, 152
		Citadel	19	Mar Elias	66
		Damascus Gate	19, 20	Mar Saba	77
		Dome of the Rock	24, 25	Masada	7, 83-87
Daliyat el-Carmel	143	Dung Gate	19, 20	Megiddo	6, 104-105
Dead Sea	80-82, 90	El Aqsa Mosque	24, 26	Meron	124
Dead Sea Scrolls	53, 81-82	Garden Tomb	47-48	Meron Golan	129
Degania	94, 121	Gethsemane	42	Metullah	126
Dimona	88	Golgotha	32, 34	Mizpeh Shalem	83
Dor	144	Israel Museum	53	Modiin	135
Dothan	103	Jaffa Gate	19, 20	Motza	133
Druze	143	Jewish Quarter	28-31	Mukhraka	142

Naaran	80	Red Sea	154	Tabgha	114
Nabateans	151	Rehovot	137	Tabor, Mount	107
Nablus	100	Revivim	152	Tantura	144
Jacob's Well	101	Rishon Le Zion	137	Tel Aviv	147
Ancient Shechem	101	Rosh Ha'Ayin	136	Tel Dan	127
Nachsholim	145	Rosh Hanikra	138	Tel Hai	126
Nahariya	138	Rosh Pina	124	Temptation, Mount of	80
Nain	107			Tiberias	111-3
Natanya	146	Safed	122-4	Timna	153-4
National Water Carrier	109, 115	Sakhne (Gan Hashlosha)	93	Tsippori	108
Nazareth	105-7	Samaria	6, 102		
Church of Annunciation	106	Samaritans	102	Um Rashrash	154
Mary's Well	106	Sartaba	90	Underwater Observatory	155
Nebi Samuel	96	Sde Boker	151		
Negba	148	Sdom	87		
Negev	74	Sdot Yam	146	Yad Mordechai	149
Neve Yaacov	96	Sea of Galilee	110	Yavne	7
		Shar HaGai	133	Yotvata	152-3
Petach Tikva	136	Shaar Hagolan	94		
		Shechem	101-2		
Qumran	81	Shiloh	97-8	Wadi Amud	114
		Shivta	151, 152	Wadi Kelt	77
		Shuafat	96	Weizman Institute	137
Ramallah	97	Solomon's Pillars	153		
Ramat Magshimim	129	Solomon's Pools	71		
Ramle	137	Sorek Cave	133, 134	Zichron Ya'acov	145
Ramon Crater	152	Susita	120	Zorah	134